WHO STOLE
MY BIBLE?

Reclaiming Scripture as a Handbook for **Resisting Tyranny**

Rev. Jennifer Butler
Foreword by Brian McLaren

PRAISE FOR *WHO STOLE MY BIBLE?*

Jennifer Butler has written a forceful manifesto of awakening to the claims of biblical faith amid our deep and costly social political crisis. Butler is deeply rooted in faith and is a major player in public issues as the head of Faith in Public Life. Her chapters in this book, time after time, show how the Bible teems with contemporaneity, both as summons and as assurance. This remarkable book reaches out to "Bible believers" even as it appeals to the most faithful impulses of "progressives." Butler's writing is personal, imaginative, accessible, and compelling. I found it to be an empowering page-turner.
 —Walter Brueggemann, Columba Theological Seminary

Jennifer Butler's Who Stole My Bible? *is a revelation. Among the saddest moments in church history were the moments when multiple streams of the church began to distance themselves from the Bible. In the zeal of the scientific age and in response to white supremacy whole church streams wrote off the Bible as defunct, old-hat, rusty, irrelevant, and the problem itself. In* Who Stole My Bible?, *Butler shows us these pervasive analyses erase the Brown, colonized, resisting skin and flesh of the writers of these ancient texts. She makes a clarion call for the progressive church to repent from its progression away from the Brown text of colonized women and men and look again— through decolonized eyes. Liberation is in these pages.*
 —Lisa Sharon Harper, author of *The Very Good Gospel* and president and founder of Freedom Road

Who Stole My Bible? *is a bold and beautiful call to every Christian to resist empire and manifest the Reign of God on earth. By brilliantly weaving together a liberative exegesis of biblical texts, a thoughtful exposition of current reality (sitz im laben) and a helpful analysis of models of leadership that work, Jennifer Butler creates a practical map for each of us to reclaim* scripture—and the Jesus to which it points—as a way to heal our broken world. This is a poignant, prophetic, and practical must-read book for all Christian leaders, clergy and lay.

—Rev. Dr. Jacqueline J. Lewis, senior minister,
Middle Collegiate Church

Jennifer Butler walks the path of faith with the grit of a soldier, compassion of a first responder, creativity of an artist, and unyielding moral voice of a prophet. This book calls to those bruised by religion to witness the healing waters of reclaimed faith while demanding long time practitioners to preach Jesus through embodied action versus shallow slogans and harsh judgment. This is the book to pass on to the spiritual exile and the overly pious believer; each will find joy and common ground in this beautifully written publication.

—Otis Moss, III, senior pastor, Trinity United Church of Christ

Rev. Jen Butler's book is a meditation on biblical stories that resonate with the truth of today. She stirs up our very human reactions mirrored in scripture and leads to the challenging need for action then . . . and now! It stirs my spirit in challenging times.

—Sister Simone Campbell, leader of NETWORK
and Nuns on the Bus,
author of Hunger for Hope

For years, I have been honored to be both a fan and friend of Rev. Jen Butler. Now, I'm thrilled to recommend her powerful, insightful, and well-written new book, Who Stole My Bible?: Reclaiming Scripture as a Handbook for Resisting Tyranny. Like Jen, I love the Bible and I lament how it is often used as a weapon of oppression instead of a handbook for liberation. Jen's new book will reintroduce you to the Bible just in time to help you take your stand—with Jen and so many tyranny resistors—in this time of such great danger and opportunity.

—Brian D. McLaren, author/speaker/activist

For years, Rev. Jennifer Butler has been a steadfast and leading voice of faith in immoral times—from church basements in Georgia to the streets and halls of power in Washington, DC. With Who Stole My Bible?*, Rev. Butler has given us a moving, personal, and energizing account of how a deep understanding of the Biblical narrative can be a transformational force for change in a society that is in desperate need of transformation.*
—Rabbi Jason Kimelman-Block, Washington director of
Bend the Arc Jewish Action

Jennifer Butler's provocative and inspiring Who Stole My Bible? *answers the spiritual and moral reckoning our country urgently demands as we endure multiple, divisive crises. Butler's understanding of her Christian faith reminds me, as a Muslim, of the values of social justice and compassion I was taught as a student at an all-boys Jesuit high school. She reveals the true path of the prophets, fierce advocates of a loving God that use faith as a shield to protect the vulnerable and a sword against the abuses of tyranny.*
—Wajahat M. Ali, *New York Times* contributing op-ed writer
and award-winning playwright

This is the book we need for "such a time as this."(Esther 4:14) Who Stole My Bible? *shows us how to take back sacred texts from the radical Christian Right. Instead of cherry-picking biblical texts to support unjust and even cruel social policy, Rev. Jennifer Butler asks us to imagine ourselves in the resistance struggles that formed the scriptures so we can see ourselves as actors in God's long work of justice and mercy as it is unfolding today. This is not the first time Christians have had to struggle to reclaim scripture. Time and again, tyrants have tried to arm themselves with scriptural warrants, violating the divine message in the process. This imaginative and engaging book says "Basta!" to that tyrannical practice. This really is a handbook for how to live the resistance with biblical imagination and courage.*
—Rev. Dr. Susan Brooks Thistlethwaite, president emerita and
professor emerita,
Chicago Theological Seminary

Too often the Bible has been used to defend the indefensible and to justify oppression, inequality, exclusion, and all sorts of ungodly things. In this book, my friend Rev. Jen Butler reclaims the Bible as a blueprint for revolution—a revolution of love and compassion and justice. This deep dive into the Holy Book is an invitation to join the ancient Story of a God who is redeeming the world, liberating the captives, breaking the yokes of oppression, and casting the mighty from their thrones. Get ready to get in the way of injustice. Get ready to get into good trouble. Get ready to join the resistance.

—Shane Claiborne, author, activist, and co-founder of Red Letter Christians

The Bible is a radical book of justice and love. The life of Jesus shows us how to act in this way. Who Stole My Bible? is a book for people who are tired of having the Bible used for oppression. Reverend Butler shows us how to take our faith and justice seriously!

—Reverend Jes Kast, United Church of Christ Pastor

Rev. Jennifer Butler provides the critical moral leadership that our nation craves at this pivotal moment in history. Who Stole My Bible? will inspire Christians to follow Jesus by working for the common good. These aren't just good words either because Rev. Butler has a strong track record of good works to back them up.

—Guthrie Graves-Fitzsimmons, author of *Just Faith: Reclaiming Progressive Christianity*

This book challenged me to see not just Scripture, but the God who inspired that Scripture in a new way. By immersing the reader into the biblical story, Rev. Butler creates opportunities for empathy and new understanding. It's truly inspired me to read the Bible with a new lens.

—Juliet Vedral, writer

Who Stole My Bible? is both a timely and timeless book for people of faith facing—and resisting—oppression, tyranny, and authoritarianism in any age. With both imagination and clear-eyed determination to restore an ethical theological voice in the public square, Butler urges us to recover our prophetic vocation for justice, and she gives us the tools in this book. This handbook is an essential companion for the protestor, preacher, and people in the pews to re-establish God's vision of radical justice, equality, and liberation that the Bible intended.

—Rev. Dr. Leah D. Schade
author of *Preaching in the Purple Zone: Ministry in the Red Blue Divide*;
co-founder of the Clergy Emergency League;
assistant professor of preaching and worship, Lexington Theological Seminary

Conservative Christians try to dismiss progressive Christians by claiming we aren't biblical. Over and over again, in her new book, Jennifer Butler proves them wrong. She firmly demonstrates how the roots of social justice are entangled with those of Christianity and our religious texts. Then, in very personal and engaging ways, she connects them to our modern reality and sends out a call for resistance. I also can't help but believe she was wearing her Ruth Bader Ginsberg dissent collar the whole time she was writing the book. I highly encourage folks to read this book and to accept her call to resist!

—Rev. Mark Sandlin, M. Div., co-founder of The Christian Left, president of ProgressiveChristianity.org admin@faithinpubliclife.org

Editing by Cara Highsmith, Highsmith Creative Services, www.highsmithcreative.com

Cover and Interior Design by Mitchell Shea

I have tried to re-create events, locales, and conversations from my memories of them.
In order to maintain their anonymity in some instances, I have changed the names of
individuals and places; I may have changed some identifying characteristics and details,
such as physical properties, occupations, and places of residence.

Default translation. Unless otherwise noted, scripture comes from:
New Revised Standard Version (NRSV) – All Scripture quoted from the New Revised Stan-
dard Version Bible, copyright © 1989 the Division of Christian Education of the National
Council of the Churches of Christ in the United States of America. Used by permission.
All rights reserved.

Also used:
New International Version (NIV) – THE HOLY BIBLE, NEW INTERNATIONAL VERSION®, NIV®
Copyright © 1973, 1978, 1984, 2011 by Biblica, Inc.® Used by permission. All rights re-
served worldwide.

ISBN-13: 978-1-7357392-0-5
ISBN eBook: 978-1-7357392-1-2

Printed in the United States of America
First Edition 14 13 12 11 10 / 10 9 8 7 6 5 4 3 2 1

CONTENTS

DEDICATION

I dedicate this book to brave and sometimes lonely Christians finding their way out of the wilderness and into the streets. May you find joy in reclaiming and resisting.

WHO STOLE MY BIBLE?

FOREWORD

I wonder if you cringe when you read these words:

> Early on in "Narrative of the Life of Frederick
> Douglass," the first of three autobiographies
> Douglass wrote over his lifetime, he recounts
> what happened—or, perhaps more accurately,
> what didn't happen—after his master, Thomas
> Auld, became a Christian believer at a Method-
> ist camp meeting. Douglass had harbored the
> hope that Auld's conversion, in August, 1832,
> might lead him to emancipate his slaves, or at
> least "make him more kind and humane." In-
> stead, Douglass writes, "If it had any effect on
> his character, it made him more cruel and hate-
> ful in all his ways." Auld was ostentatious about
> his piety—praying "morning, noon, and night,"
> participating in revivals, and opening his home
> to travelling preachers—but he used his faith
> as license to inflict pain and suffering upon his
> slaves. "I have seen him tie up a lame young
> woman, and whip her with a heavy cowskin
> upon her naked shoulders, causing the warm
> red blood to drip; and, in justification of the
> bloody deed, he would quote this passage of
> Scripture—'He that knoweth his master's will,
> and dœth it not, shall be beaten with many
> stripes.' "

Earlier today, when I came across this story in a powerful article
by journalist Michael Luo (*The New Yorker,* September 2, 2020),
I felt like I'd been punched in the gut. *There it is again,* I thought.
*Another human being harmed by a vicious man armed with a
Bible.*

I grew up with the Bible. I sang songs about the Bible in
church ("The B-I-B-L-E, yes, that's the book for me!"). I memorized

verses from the Bible and won prizes in Sunday school. My dad led us in (almost) daily Bible reading at the dinner table. The Bible was as much a part of our daily diet as mashed potatoes or eggs and toast. I went to Bible camp in the summer. By the time I was a teenager, I was trying to read the Bible through every year, although it often took me longer than a year. I can't guess how many hours of sermons I heard on the Bible by the time I was eighteen because we were a family that went to church three times a week most weeks. Even if you discount the times I fell asleep or daydreamed, I learned a lot more Bible as a teenager than many adult preachers I've met since.

When I went to college to become an English teacher, I felt that my immersion in the Bible had taught me a lot of the skills of literary criticism, equipping me with a strong sense of plot, poetics, parallelism, and more. I eventually left teaching to become a pastor, and in twenty-four years in the pastorate, I probably inflicted upon others even more sermons as I had ever listened to growing up! For almost every one of those sermons, I spent hours in Bible study.

In the years since leaving the pastorate, I've written over a dozen books, all dealing with the Bible, including one overview of the whole Bible from "Genesis to maps," as we Bible nerds like to say.

So I have a lot of history with the Bible. And I can tell you, there is no book out there on the Bible like this one by Jen Butler.

Although I don't know Jen quite as well as I know the Bible, I have known her for years. I have seen her at work as an activist for social justice, as the founding director of one of our nation's best faith-rooted justice organizations, as the leader of the White House Council on Faith and Neighborhood Partnerships, as a public speaker, and as an organizer. I've seen her on TV, read her op-eds, and marched beside her in protests, confronting social injustice. I also am her colleague in the Auburn Senior Fellows, a close community of multi-faith leaders collaborating for justice and peace.

I know what a lot of people don't know: that Jen has an MDiv from Princeton Theological Seminary, and she is an ordained Presbyterian minister. So I know she possesses real grounding in the Bible herself.

What I didn't know is how creatively she could write, and how wisely she would approach this subject.

I was expecting a book about how the Bible has been abused and how it can be better used. That would have been good. But Jen has given us something even better. Instead of writing about the Bible in general, Jen guides us deep into nine specific passages of Scripture. Instead of *telling* us how the Bible can be better used in theory, she *shows us* in practice.

Preachers could use this book as a prompt for nine amazing sermons of their own. Study groups could do the same. Seminary classrooms could make this a required text. Normal people like you and me could read it to help us "take heed how we hear" when we hear a preacher say something outlandish.

Because do not doubt this for a minute: the same kind of harmful, dangerous, destructive, abhorrent use of the Bible that Frederick Douglass experienced is still happening today.

Thank God for Jen Butler and for all the teachers, preachers, and students of the Bible who can now, with her help, show us a better way.

—Brian D. McLaren (brianmclaren.net)

INTRODUCTION

The fight for justice has taken me from rural one-room churches in South Georgia to immaculate cathedrals in the heart of New York. I have traveled hundreds of miles with dedicated religious leaders, such as Rev. Dr. William Barber II, Sister Simone Campbell, Rabbi Jason Kimelman-Block, and Imam Horsed Noah. We mobilized faith communities around voting rights, economic equality, health care access, the protection of immigrant and religious minorities, LGBTQ rights, criminal justice reform, and many other issues. I have stood in the halls of Congress and been arrested for grounding my feet in the house of the people, a house where true and just decisions are supposed to be made.

I have come to understand that my feet are not solely grounded on the polished marble of congressional halls or the dusty roads leading to a border wall. I am able to stand in these places and engage in resistance because I am grounded in the sacred texts of my faith. When my feet grow weary from this standing and walking and resisting, I am held up by Scripture.

This grounding of resistance, especially in the biblical narratives, has been at times a lonely journey as I heard the voice of God but lacked a community that could help me express what I knew in my heart to be true. It was not a sudden Damascus Road experience, like that of Paul. It was a slow journey that took me from Sunday school certainty, to doubt, to cynicism, then to renewal, hope, and power. The grounding of my resistance to injustice, to the genuine tyrannies of our time, has come to me from joining and sharing my lived faith with others as we have walked and stood and prayed for justice. This is where I feel closest to God. As a white, cisgender woman, I learned to approach the biblical texts with humility, listening, and learning as I travel this road of advocating for social justice. That is the journey to which I invite you.

The Bible that inspired Civil Rights leaders was not the Bible I heard about on the nightly news growing up. I get asked: What happened to that more progressive religious voice that challenged racism and economic inequality? In the 1970s and 1980s the New Right—galvanized by white supremacist presidential candidate Barry Goldwater—organized the Christian Right to protect the right of private schools to discriminate against people of color. Progressive religious leaders failed to counter them for two reasons: First, as Christian Right groups organized a backlash to denominational social justice programs, social justice programs and spokespeople were defunded and muzzled over time. But more important, some took the First Amendment phrase "separation of Church and State" to mean that religious viewpoints should not be expressed in the public square. We often followed the lead of secular allies who preferred to use legal strategies and whose emphasis on "separating Church and State" was mistaken at times to mean religious perspectives should not be offered as part of public policy debates. As a result, those of us committed to antiracism and to LGBTQ and women's rights lost faith in our own voices. But in a democracy, voices from all religious or nonreligious viewpoints should be welcome. The problem wasn't that conservative religious voices were weighing in, but rather that public debates had become dominated exclusively by theologically misguided, nativist, and exclusivist voices. Our biblically-grounded public voices were needed to counter such views, but we were often absent or outgunned and drowned out.

Too many, including myself, have experienced sexism, sexual harassment, and sexual abuse at the hands of Christian leaders and institutions that used immoral perversions of scriptural teaching to validate their behavior. The LGBTQ community has been dehumanized and demonized by those who resort to a handful of biblical texts to support their positions that are often misread and lifted out of context. Racism has been justified scripturally for hundreds of years in this country by white supremacists, even up until the very moment I am writing this. Non-Christians have been targeted with suspicion, hate speech, and violence. We have been trained to believe that such behavior is even grounded in Scripture.

It is no surprise to me that the ranks of spiritual "nones" are increasing as young people disillusioned by the Church's many sins of exclusion and abuse vote with their feet. In my twenties, I considered walking away from Christianity and my call to ministry because of the sexual harassment and misogyny I encountered in the Church and misuse of biblical texts. I cannot blame others for turning away. But I offer this: for me, my healing and spiritual well-being depended on my reclaiming the Bible, and thus my faith, rather than allowing bad actors to force me out.

It might surprise you to know that a group of Muslim women inspired me to reclaim my Christianity. I was organizing in the global women's movement with religious women of all faiths working to counter religious extremism and violence against women. At one point, my coalition helped sponsor an event for Muslim women in a chapel across from the United Nations building. I cleared the Communion table there to use as a panelist table—an image of global communion I still carry with me. Midway through the presentation, the Saudi Arabian ambassador and his security detail burst into the room, creating a disturbance in the entryway to physically intimidate the speakers who were criticizing Saudi government policies. As the panelist faltered, the audience immediately rose to its feet and launched into a five-minute round of applause blocking the delegation with their bodies. The shaken speaker was able to continue her presentation with their enemy hidden from view— the women sitting by the door refused to sit down until the interlopers left humiliated. That moment inspired and challenged me to follow the example of Muslim women who risked being arrested or physically attacked to reclaim their voice, their social and political equality, and their faith.

As I continue to march in demonstrations against the violence of racism in this country, I have ever more deeply come to comprehend the importance of knowing that the people in the Bible were not white. That is, they were not of European ethnicity with a light-skin pigment, despite our depictions of Jesus as a light-skinned, blond-haired, blue-eyed man. There are no white people in the Bible, though so many white people act as if they own the Bible. We don't.

White, ruling-class Europeans appropriated the Hebrew Bible and the Christian Scriptures and read themselves into the text. They abused these sacred texts to justify horrific violence against Jews, and to justify their own empire building, which they had the gall to deem a "Holy Crusade." Violence against women was justified over and over by narrow and misogynistic readings of these texts. The Holocaust and the murder of 6 million Jews did not fall from the sky. It was the product of centuries of antisemitism produced by this misreading and consequent mistreatment.

The slave trade was biblically justified, over and over, along with a scriptural justification for slavery preached by white preachers at the enslaved Africans. The portions of Scripture that told a different story were heartlessly cut out of Bibles so the enslaved would not learn that God staged the Exodus and set people free from slavery.

But those who had been enslaved saw clearly what the Bible conveyed. They knew exactly who and what Pharaoh was, and who Jesus of Nazareth was, and who exactly hung Jesus on a cross to die. And they knew, and their descendants know, that Jesus rose.

Today we face fundamental threats to democracy, the system of governance that protects the fundamental biblical teaching that human beings are created in God's image and worthy of dignity and respect.

White supremacy, never gone from this society, has gained momentum in the wake of a number of successful rollbacks and challenges to legal victories, which were won by the Civil Rights Movement, via an overtly racist presidency.[1] Economic inequality has reached its highest level since the 1920s[2] as the wealthy take advantage of their power and influence. And let us be very clear. The wealthy are overwhelmingly white and those who are systematically economically disadvantaged are people of color.

The Fourth Estate—the media—has been undermined by the influence of money. Most media outlets are owned by for-profit corporations and funded by corporate advertising, which seeks to fill a twenty-four-hour news cycle with sensationalized and polarizing content that we voraciously consume. Social media has left us vulnerable to trolling and misinformation campaigns, both domestic and foreign.[3]

Money in politics and a new type of gerrymandering advanced in the nineties is close to locking political power in the hands of one party: the Republicans.[4] America is one election away from a one-party system. Democratic norms are being undermined and political corruption abounds. Dark money is enabling a few to enrich themselves at the expense of the health of our planet by denying climate science and turning a blind eye to environmental devastation.

The Voting Rights Act has been gutted and the votes of people of color have been systematically undermined just as they were in the Jim Crow era. Michelle Alexander has helped us see that there is a New Jim Crow created in large part through the policies that have led to the mass incarceration of young Black men.[5]

Our nation's prison and jail population has quintupled in thirty years, leaving us with the highest incarceration rate in the world. A third of Black men have felony records—due in large part to a racially biased, brutal drug war—and have been relegated to a permanent second-class status. Plans are being made to incarcerate and deport millions of immigrants. Refugees are now unwelcome on the shores of a nation built by refugees of famine and religious violence.

The precious value of religious freedom is being used as a weapon to deny LGBTQ people jobs and housing, just as it was once used to defend slavery and segregation.[6] Rather than using religious freedom as a shield, Christians are using it as a sword.

In the midst of a global pandemic, some cry out for a false "freedom" to reopen our economy against advice from public health experts, which places at risk the freedom of tens of millions of precious human beings—a majority being from communities of color and frontline workers—who are forced to participate in an economy while risking their lives and the lives of those they love. Individualism is triumphing over care for neighbors and freedom over equality as communities of color are hardest hit.[7] Rather than care for our health and livelihoods at the same time, our president and many of our governors have politicized a pandemic and deny its very existence.

The usurping of moral norms, like human dignity and loving your neighbor, is at the root of so much chaos. These beliefs are being undermined in favor of unbridled greed, ethnic nationalism, and xenophobia. A large percentage of white Christians is marching to the drumbeat of white nationalism[8] and leading the way in the corruption of our values.

Given all of this, nothing could be more important than reclaiming this radical book called the Bible and acting to make its vision for radical justice, equality, and liberation a reality.

The effort to control and misrepresent faith is an age-old tactic used by tyrants. Abolitionists went up against slaveholders who cherry-picked certain verses to uphold white supremacy. The Confessing Church movement sought in vain to stop Nazis from taking over the German Church and replacing its doctrines with Nazi beliefs of white racial superiority.[9] LGBTQ people of faith have consistently and successfully defined themselves as children of God and have refused to be defined as "sinners" by a handful of misinterpreted biblical texts.

We should soberly consider that powerful people and institutions will try to control faith—exactly because it is powerful. They might, like slaveholders did, cut out portions of the Bible—the Book of Exodus, first and foremost—known to incite slave rebellions.[10] They might simply never preach on the most important texts. Or they might misinterpret certain passages so as to make you submit and undermine your spiritual authority. This is why it is critical to read Scripture through the lens of the oppressed. They have the clearest perspective. As a white cisgender woman, I know I cannot read Scripture alone. As we march and pray and sing and lobby and sign petitions, we learn together what true biblical justice can look like in action. Rabbi Abraham Heschel famously said that when he went to Selma, Alabama, to march with Rev. Dr. Martin Luther King Jr., "I felt my feet were praying."

For me, Scripture is at the same time "God-Breathed" and an account of an imperfect people struggling to draw near to what is holy and good. Scripture was written by people with often-flawed perspectives, translated by people with agendas, and is preached by people with blind spots. The overarching theme of Scripture is God's intervention in history as One who hears the groans of oppressed people and acts. We understand the Bible best when we try to join that story.

If we want to prevent tyrants from seizing power, we must prevent them from becoming gods. It is easy for them to become gods when they control faith and Scripture. By sharing how your beliefs lead you to oppose oppression, you will be more fully equipped to bend the arc of the universe toward justice. Whether you do this in your church, your family, your social circle, or in the public square, know that your theological, scriptural-based voice is powerful, especially when joined with others.

In doing so, you stand on the shoulders of giants. Writing about Sojourner Truth, historian Imani Perry observed that Truth had three goals: end slavery, advance women, and reclaim the Gospel.[11] When Southern white clergy argued for patience and gradual change, Rev. Dr. Martin Luther King Jr., from a jail cell in Birmingham, Alabama, made a theological case for urgency and nonviolent resistance: "But the judgement of God is on the church as never before."[12] Drawing on liberationist themes of Exodus and the prophets, the Civil Rights Movement brought an end to Jim Crow.

The Book of Hebrews in the New Testament teaches that we are part of a great cloud of witnesses. Biblical witnesses form the stories that are given to us in Scripture. But there are many other, postbiblical witnesses recorded in history books. I seek in this book to connect the two—biblical and postbiblical leaders whose work has shown just what can and should be done to resist tyranny.

I have arranged this book around biblical stories that help us see the overall arc of Scripture as a call to resist tyranny. Each chapter imaginatively retells a biblical story, then connects the story with a prophetic religious response from history or recent events. I draw on the work of political scientists and historians whose analysis offers us tools to identify and counter the creeping shadow of authoritarianism in our world today. By drawing a parallel between ancient and more recent stories of faith resistance to tyranny, I hope to draw out key tactics that faith communities can use to follow God's charge to liberate the oppressed: truth-telling, public theological debate, ministries of radical compassion, nonviolent direct action, lament, prophetic imagination, symbol, and ritual.

I invite you into a walk through several key turning points in Scripture and experience them as a radical call, in a world of brutal empires, to establish a society where all human beings can flourish and be treated with equal dignity. This alternate vision for how we live together is critical today as American democracy (never fully realized) is now fundamentally threatened.

I weave these stories and lessons together because I believe that being hopeful at this moment in history requires us to see ourselves in a long line of spiritual activists who have worked to liberate the oppressed.

These spiritual ancestors live in us through their stories. They walk with us, weep with us, shout with us, and sometimes shout *at* us. They will help us through these troubled times. We are not alone in this journey with all of its twists and turns, ups and downs, steps forward and steps backward. Our ancestors whisper in our ears that we must take hope. We must continue their work. They faced far worse and overcame impossible odds.

This is the way we can build the "kin-dom" of God as *mujerista* theologian Ada Maria Isasi-Diaz said, and the way we can do the work of God's *libertad*. Jesus spoke of the coming kingdom of God that would usher in God's vision of a world without oppressive hierarchies. Ada Maria Isasi-Diaz has proposed the language of "kin-dom" as a helpful way to further disrupt the gendered language and the church's failure to reckon with the radical nature of what Jesus actually proposed. *Kin-dom* is the interconnected community, based on the experience of Latinx, that works to create God's justice in the world.

If you are wary of Scripture, this book is for you. If you love Scripture, but sense that what you have been taught in church doesn't always add up, this book is for you. If you are on the verge of leaving your church because of the intolerance and bigotry you see among Christians, this book is for you. If you want to learn how to connect your faith and understanding of Scripture with your commitment to build a more just and compassionate world, this book is for you.

I hope that in reading this book, you catch a vision of yourself as part of generations of faith communities who resisted tyranny in impossible circumstances, when the future looked bleak. I hope that this effort to explore what the text means for us today inspires your own journey to look at Scripture with new eyes and discern what you are being called to do and say in this moment in history.

CHAPTER 1
Grounding Your Resistance in Scripture

By some amazing but vastly creative spiritual insight the slave undertook the redemption of a religion that the master had profaned in his midst.
—Howard Thurman

In the months before I left home to study Scripture and theology at Princeton Theological Seminary, a friend of my father's warned him that my learning the tools of "biblical exegesis" might undermine the "authority" of Scripture and cause me to lose faith. Indeed, many fear that using history, sociology, and textual analysis to understand the context in which Scripture was written might somehow shake one's faith.

On the contrary, these studies took me deeper in my faith. They enlivened the texts and sent me on a renewed spiritual journey. Often they confirmed things I knew in my gut, but didn't have the self-assurance to claim. As a child, I had always wondered how we came by these stories. Learning how they were written and assembled and under what circumstances the stories were told made them all the more exciting. Here we had the opportunity to converse with people from centuries ago about their journey with God. The more I knew about the people and their language, the better. How did they live? What other stories would they have heard? What would these words have meant in all of their nuances to a person living at that time? We need not see Scripture as handed to us straight from

God to believe that it is authoritative in its ability to inspire us and convey deeper truths about the human struggle to be who God truly calls us to be.

No one needs a graduate degree to read Scripture in this way. Harriet Tubman and Sojourner Truth were illiterate freed slaves and yet they interpreted Scripture with an accuracy that white slaveholders lacked. Their confidence in their own interpretation of Scripture gave them courage and conviction to risk their lives for their own freedom, as well as that of others.

Studying Scripture did cause me to wrestle with my faith, but this wrestling ultimately made my faith even stronger.

The most joyful moments in my life have come while watching people come to terms with the true meaning of biblical texts by wrestling with them in study, prayer, and activism. In recent years, I've seen this transformation at some of our press conferences and rallies. While intended to pressure elected officials, these have taken on the feeling of religious revival.

In 2017, Republicans attempted to remove 20 million people from Affordable Care Act enrollment and cripple the legislation beyond repair. In forty-eight hours, Rev. Barber and I called a moral state of emergency and rallied faith leaders to oppose the "Death Bill." Days later, three hundred faithful activists gathered at the Capitol with holy texts and health care testimonials in hand. Hundreds of us jammed into the hallways outside the office of Congressional House Majority Leader Paul Ryan. When denied entry, we loudly held a revival in the corridor because we knew he was in there. For hours we read from our sacred texts and prayed for those who had died or would be killed by this bill. People prayed, sang, wept. A Catholic lay leader led us in the Lord's Prayer, hoping to appeal to the Catholic political leader inside. An imam spoke, citing the Koran. A Rabbi read Torah. At the end, we left our holy texts at the representative's door. The stack was piled three feet high.

Departing from that scene, the soles of my feet felt bruised. The rush of adrenaline had made me hungry to the point of feeling dizzy. I was emotionally spent. Stumbling away from this intense experience of the sacred, I found myself beside a woman who looked dazed as well. Her eyes were open wide and had a faraway look. Ever the organizer, I asked if she was okay and knew where to go next. She looked at me, and in a stunned voice, she said, "I feel like I just found my voice. I never knew how to speak from my faith, though it compelled me to act. Now I'm learning how to speak again." She wandered off in what I sensed was a cloud of glory.

That image, which I feel I can never quite fully convey, brings me to tears as much as my recollection of John McCain's thumbs-down on the Senate floor after a summer of protest. That moment miraculously ended the deadly attempt to take health care away from 20 million people. But that moment was born of months of protests that raised the moral costs of such actions. So many had stepped out in faith, knowing the odds were entirely against us. But we won.

I did not always have such a community. Growing up in the South, I found that what Jesus said in Scripture was not often lived out in my white, well-heeled church on Peachtree Street in Atlanta, Georgia. I took Jesus' mission statement in Luke 4:18 quite literally: "The Spirit of the Lord is upon me, because he has anointed me to bring good news to the poor...and to let the oppressed go free." When the conservative white Christians around me said they took the Bible literally, I never heard them talk about freedom for the oppressed.

I felt lost. I read Scripture for myself, but what I read did not match up with what I was hearing from the pulpit and from the Moral Majority.

I had been one of the first children in the South to attend integrated public schools. No, I was not six in 1954 when the US Supreme Court decided *Brown* v. *Board of Education of Topeka*. It took twenty years for Supreme Court justices to hold the South to that decision through court-mandated enforcement.

Many, maybe most, white Christians pulled their kids out of public schools and into all-white Christian academies. In 1963, The Lovett School, loosely affiliated with the Episcopal Diocese of Atlanta, rejected the applications of three Black students, including the son of Martin Luther King Jr.[1] These Christian

3

Academies in Atlanta, the one I later attended among them, remain over 90 percent white to this day in a county that is 40 percent African American.[2]

At the time, I did not know these things. History books taught that we had overcome our racist history. And yet occasionally I would hear the "N-word" from people I knew and loved. Looking back, I rewind the childhood tapes and I realize that was when they were talking about their support for Lester Maddox, the staunch segregationist who served as governor from 1967 to 1971, the early years of my life.

At fourteen, I decided to follow Jesus in my own right. I prayed, *I am not sure you are there, but I will follow you and find out. Please save us from nuclear Armageddon. Please change the hearts of those who are racist. And please help my nerdy self through high school.*

I was a born-again Christian at the exact moment that the Christian Right was taking off. All of my friends started supporting Ronald Reagan. Yet for me, Jesus' teachings on peacemaking and the two thousand verses on poverty drove me toward Jimmy Carter.

It would be years before I met other Christians like me— many of whom live in Georgia, where Faith in Public Life is currently organizing against voter suppression, gun violence, hate crimes, and LGBTQ discrimination. I was isolated for too long, trying to follow God, but without a community and without a theology that could help me speak to my beliefs. My heart goes out to those who are now in that same boat. This is one of the main reasons I built Faith in Public Life. Not only do I want to help pass just laws, I want people to know the joy God actually offers us through the struggle for liberation.

I was lucky to enroll in seminary, where I learned the tools of biblical exegesis and theology, particularly liberation theologies, which were more rooted in Scripture than the theology I was taught growing up. During the 1950s and 1960s, Latin-American Catholics began to develop liberation theology. In 1971, the Peruvian priest Fr. Gustavo Gutiérrez wrote one of the movement's defining books, *A Theology of Liberation,* and coined the term "liberation theology." In the United States during the sixties and seventies, Black, feminist, womanist (Black women), *mujerista* (Latinx women), Palestinian, Asian, LGBTQ, and many other theologies were developed. All of them are based on the belief that the God revealed in Scripture is the "God of the Oppressed"—the God who calls for an end to oppression and who reveals Godself to those experiencing tyranny. God can therefore be best understood by hearing the experience of God from those living under the boot of systems of oppression.

It was not until I became the executive director of Faith in Public Life in 2005, however, that my deep love of the Scriptures and the work of peace and justice came together in a profound way.

In 2006, Faith in Public Life began to work with faith leaders to amplify their voices in the media in hopes of contesting decades of damaging Christian right dominance in the media. We built bridges across all kinds of divides. We were multifaithed, working with religious leaders of both political parties. We didn't all agree on every single issue, but we were able to team up on most because of our common values.

At first, there was little agreement on marriage equality, but we found common cause in opposing discrimination. Abortion was another flashpoint, but we aligned in striving for a world in which pregnancy could be almost always a cause for celebration. We advocated for health care for all Americans, especially women who often lacked the care they needed to plan pregnancies and get the maternity care they needed. And we worked to end pregnancy discrimination, raise the minimum wage, and ensure access to health care and education. We agreed that criminalizing women and doctors would not get us anywhere.

Today we work with fifty thousand religious leaders around the country and we have offices and deep networks in four states. Every day we are winning policy victories that demonstrate the compassionate and just world order imagined in our holy texts.

Our work of resistance needs to be rooted in the practice of compassion and of empathy for the excluded other. In the same way, if we deeply empathize with the actors in the biblical stories, so much so that we imagine ourselves part of the story, a connection is formed that will ground our work.

This is how Jesus of Nazareth told stories in the form of parables to those who gathered around him. A parable is a story that invites you to imagine yourself in the shoes of the other. Like most stories, particularly those full of compelling sights and sounds and symbols, parables speak to you as you move through life.

One really good story for showing this method is that of the Good Samaritan. Jesus begins: "A man Jericho was going down from Jerusalem to Jericho, and he fell into the hands of robbers, who stripped him, beat him, and went away leaving him half dead (Luke 10:30b)."

Oh no, you say to yourself, *there's a crisis. What will happen?*

As a modern reader, there is a lot of context missing from this story. If we take time to learn it, we go deeper in our understanding. For example: I am told by those who have traveled this road that it is full of hairpin turns dropping twenty thousand feet into the Dead Sea. It is a dangerous road, perfect for thieves wanting to ambush travelers.

Next, a couple of influential religious leaders pass by. We feel a sense of relief, believing the man would be rescued; but, no, they ignore the suffering man. Now we are outraged. *Why did they ignore him?!*

"But a Samaritan, while travelling, came near him; and when he saw him, he was moved with pity (Luke 10:33)."

Not knowing much about Samaritans as a child, I thought "Samaritan" meant "a good person." But if you lived in that time, you would know how Jews and Samaritans disliked each other. Once we know this, we realize we are meant to fill in "Samaritan" with a category or name of someone you dislike. Whoa! Now the parable is about more than being a nice person. It's about confronting our prejudices. About helping those we dislike or regard with suspicion. Jesus forces the lawyer who questioned him to think, *I need to be more like this person I have categorically rejected.*

The story is surprising, but as you go through your days and weeks, you begin to see the parable in your current context. You might find yourself angered by a political opponent, confronted by someone of a different political party, religion, race, sexuality, or socio-economic status. Can you show them respect and compassion? Would you risk your own well-being to help them? Should our laws reflect the values of the Good Samaritan or of those who passed by on the other side? Or do you believe our biblical values irrelevant when it comes to how our society is governed?

This way of grounding our resistance in the Bible is not just cherry-picking a good verse to quote in our speeches or comments to the press. It is a way of growing our movement in insight and compassion as we imagine ourselves in the story, identifying with the challenges of that moment. We can become the biblical actors and, in doing so, find ourselves in the story God has been trying to tell humanity for a very long time. The Bible truly becomes the Living Word, speaking to us now in our own social and political context.

I am also learning from a Jewish tradition called *midrash.* Vanessa Lovelace defines *midrash* as "a Jewish mode of interpretation that not only engages the words of the text, behind the text, and beyond the text, but also focuses on each letter, and the words left unsaid by each line." *Midrash* extrapolates from Scripture, building a story around what is written so as to flesh out what might have transpired between the lines.

The ancient contemplative practice of *Lectio Divina*—the belief that God speaks to us as we pray and ruminate on the ancient text—also inspires the way I read Scripture. *Lectio* is not study and analysis. It is more "hearty" than "heady," as one expert put it.[3] It is a different way of encountering God through prayerful meditation of the Scripture, listening to what the words say to your heart in this moment. Read the text three times aloud or listen as someone else does so. Note words or feelings that stand out to you, that speak to your soul in the moment. Rather than being merely a source of information about how to live, Scripture becomes, quite literally, a meeting place for a personal encounter with the Living God. Years of doing *Lectio Divina* inspired me to meditate on these biblical stories as I struggle to understand these times we are in. This reflection is what I will share with you in these pages.

Each chapter concludes with questions meant to help you connect the reading of the text to your current historic and political context. Hopefully, these questions give you the opportunity to grapple with what God is saying to you in these stories. Maybe you end up with more questions than answers. No worries! Follow the questions—let them be your guide.

I hope the texts will give you courage for the facing of this hour in our nation's history. I hope these stories will empower you to move from intent to action. I hope they give you courage to speak, whether to friends and family or in the public square. Your voice as a Christian, respectful of all faiths and ethical traditions, is desperately needed so all may live in dignity and peace.

CHAPTER 2
Finding the Road to True Democracy

For now, let us simply observe that the assault on human dignity is one of the prime goals of the visitation of fear, a prelude to the domination of the mind and the triumph of power.
—— Wole Soyinka

Steps from the entryway of the Creation Museum in Petersburg, Kentucky, is a life-sized diorama of two prehistoric children playing by a waterfall after Adam and Eve were expelled from the Garden of Eden. Dinosaurs cavort nearby, their animatronic mechanisms turning them into pleasant companions. Genesis Answers, the organization that created the museum, spent 27 million dollars to prove that the Genesis creation story is "scientifically accurate." Dinosaurs were created on the sixth day of creation just six thousand years ago, rather than hundreds of millions of years in the past.[1] If this sounds surprising, a 2019 Gallup Poll revealed that 40 percent of Americans share this viewpoint.[2]

Biblical inerrantists lament that the modern world does not take Scripture seriously, that "secular" and scientific claims undermine the truth of Scripture and, potentially, the very existence of God. It seems their faith is contingent on proving the Genesis creation story is scientific. They miss the fact that the creation story seeks to convey something far more important and spiritually satisfying than a scientific account of how we came to be. Genesis wants to tell us what kind of God created us, not how we were created. The God introduced in these first chapters of the Bible was unlike any other in the ancient world. This vision of God paved the way for today's concepts of human rights and democracy.

To understand the opening stories of Genesis, we must know that in the ancient world human life was cheap. Capricious, powerful gods governed the earth enslaving or destroying human life to satisfy their own selfish desires. Emperors who claimed to be gods, or at least blessed and enthroned by them, conquered, enslaved, and conscripted human beings to serve imperial designs. Near East creation stories confirmed that reality.

Then an alternative story came into that world and it radically altered the worldview and existential possibilities of anyone who heard it.

I invite you to hear the story of creation from the viewpoint of a young boy of a conquered tribe who is hearing it for the very first time. Then we will connect this story to another boy on the border between Mexico and the United States.

Our Past: A New Creation Story

"In the beginning . . ." I overheard the old man say this as he warmed himself in front of the fire. The men were telling stories to wind down from the day. Mother warned me, "Hurry home. There is a curfew."

Father used to begin many of his bedtime stories with those words. I stopped in my tracks, thinking about the last time I saw him. He held my shoulders and looked into my eyes: "I will be back soon, I promise."

But he did not return from the battle that day. Many fathers are missing. Now foreign soldiers occupy our town. One is living in our home and Mother is forced to feed him with the little we have. Soon I will be drafted to build temples or fight wars. My neighbors, who once called out in greeting as I passed, now keep their eyes down.

The embers popped and settled. It startled me back to myself. I studied the men's faces. Some of them I have seen. Others, including the storyteller, were nomads. They were in town to trade.

The older of the nomads smiled gently and continued, "In the beginning, God created the heavens and the earth."

Ah, this one. I used to ask Father to tell me scary stories at night by the warmth of the fire. I loved this one about Marduk, who created the earth and human beings from the slain body of his main foe, Tiamat. I didn't mind feeling fearful as long as I was snuggled next to Father. Now that he is gone, this story gives me nightmares. Marduk will soon burst out of the sky in his flaming chariot pulled by his team: Killer, Crusher, Unyielder, and Fleet. From the blood and bones of Tiamat, he will create human beings to be his slaves. The gods, their armies, the blood, and my missing father are all too real now.

No one ever questions Marduk's rule. It is said that he can hear everything.[3]

A chill went down my spine and I turned to leave but paused as the man said, "And God saw that it was good." Good? There was nothing good in the tale Father told me. Only violence.

I listened longer. This new god creates with just a word— no blood, no war.

I sat on a rock nearby. The man continued, his eyes sparkling with the shimmering light of the torches around him.

God created humankind in his own image,
in the image of God he created them;
male and female he created them;
God saw it was good. (Gen. 1:27)

The first time the nomad said this, he spoke it. The second time, he sang it in a deep, joyful voice. The listeners grew still. They stared into the fire, dreaming. I knew that look. I see it in my mother's eyes whenever she touches the necklace Father gave her before he left for the battle. That look is love. Hope, even.

Humans created in God's likeness. Not from the bones of dead monsters from the war. And not to serve the gods and bear the burden of hard work. The man said it was more than good. It was "very good."

The man looked at me with gentle eyes. No one had done that in a very long time.

Suddenly I heard the clank of metal. The soldiers were on patrol. I was doing nothing wrong, but still I thought, *This story is treason.* I could not put words to it, but I knew somehow this story was dangerous to those who occupied the town. I ran home. Mother was angry that I was late. I just looked into her eyes and, for the first time since the war, I melted in her arms and we held each other tight.

UNDERSTANDING THE TEXT

Creation stories exist in every culture and throughout history. They seek to convey profound truths rather than history or science. The most famous creation story in the Near East during the time the Genesis story surfaced would have been the *Enuma Elish* (Akkadian for "when above"), written during the Babylonian Dynasty (1894–1595 BCE).[4] Jeremiah Unterman in *Justice for All: How the Jewish Bible Revolutionized Ethics*, shows how a comparison between the two stories can take us deeper in our knowledge of who God is with dramatic implications for how we live together. These deep truths conveyed in the biblical creation story ground my faith far more than any scientific inquiry could ever offer.

The *Enuma Elish* is a bloody story of warring gods who murder each other for trivial reasons. The hero, Marduk, murders his mother goddess and tears her body in two. Out of half of her body he creates the heavens. He uses the skin as the firmament to ensure her waters do not escape. With the other half, he establishes earth. Marduk then kills another god and out of his blood creates humans to serve the gods.[5]

While the *Enuma Elish* story, at first glance, seems vastly different from our Genesis creation account, it actually shares many traits that suggest the original storytellers deliberately mirrored this story to propose a contrasting worldview. The opening words of the tale mention both the heavens and earth. Water is the stuff of creation: the mother goddess in *Enuma Elish* is the salt ocean. Creation occurs through divine speech. The creation of the heavens, firmament, dry land, stars, humans, all occurs in the same order. Divine rest follows.[6]

But it is the differences between the two stories that reveal the biblical account's true meaning. In the *Enuma Elish*, creation occurs through violent and unjustified conflict. But in Genesis, God's commands bring order and harmony. There is no violence—in fact, the biblical ideal (Gen. 1:29-30) is vegetarianism. Creation is pronounced "good."[7]

Wind is present in both stories. But in the *Enuma Elish*, the wind is commanded to bring about the mother goddess's bloody end. In Genesis, the wind (Hebrew *ruach*) or spirit of God "flutters" over the face of the waters, which conjures the image of a mother eagle "fluttering" over its young (Deut. 32:11).[8] God is nurturing, even maternal in nature. While compassionate, the God of Genesis rules nature. The gods of the *Enuma Elish* are part of nature—they give birth; they can be controlled by magic; they die.

The creation of humanity in Genesis is dramatically different. In the *Enuma Elish*, humans are made out of the blood of an evil god. In the Bible, the human is made in the image of God (Gen. 1:26-27). The ethical message here is clear: humans are blessed by God to be good rulers, not slaves (Gen. 1:26). In verse 29, God commands humans to be vegetarian because "the ethical purpose of God's nonviolent creation is to lead to a world without bloodshed." We are to be good rulers and stewards and, as Jeremiah Unterman, resident scholar at the Herzl Institute, says, "not eat our subjects."[9]

Relationships between the sexes are also nonviolent. The image of the biblical God refers to all men and women equally. While Eve has been presented historically as a derivative of Adam and the "lesser sex," Genesis 2 (the second creation account) conveys that a *ha-'adam* ("earth creature") is created from the earth, *ha-'adamah*.[10] This earth creature remains sexless until the differentiation of female from male occurs in Genesis 2:21–23. God makes humans (Hebrew: *adamah*), then makes male (Hebrew: *Adam*) and female (Hebrew: *Eva*) from this original gender-neutral human. These male and female humans are then told to be good partners, to be each other's "helpers." The Hebrew word used here (*ezer*) conveys throughout Scripture someone of equal or greater importance, not a servant. God is also described in this way. In Exodus, we see women like Miriam, Deborah, and Huldah who are "prophetesses"—evidence of a tradition among followers of Moses that brought women into leadership despite a surrounding patriarchal culture.

The concept of Sabbath is revolutionary. No scholar has provided any evidence for a day of rest in any other ancient society. The Jewish Bible invented the weekend. "This concept of the Sabbath rest had a democratizing influence upon society. All were equal for one full day a week (and on certain holidays) and no one could require anybody else to work on that day."[11] This was the first labor law, concludes Unterman.

The political and economic implications of the biblical creation account cannot be underestimated in terms of their impact on all of history. God steps into a world where exploitation is the norm, where conquest and domination are the order of the day, and where human despots rule with the backing of powerful and brutal gods. God steps in and says, "Enough." All creation must be treated with dignity and respect. Such a view of God was bound to have a democratizing effect.

No longer would this community be ruled by autocrats—for all were loved by God, all were equal, creation was good, and none were created to be enslaved.

America Today: An Outdated Vision of Humanity

A little boy sits, huddled on the floor of a cage in what feels like a refrigerator. There are seven other boys in his cage. He does not know where his mother is. They have taken her. He calls out to see if she is in one of the cages. There are so many.

At night he dreams of his father, imagining he is there holding him and telling him bedtime stories. His father never came home from work. They found his body by the river.

His mother knew why: his father had refused to join the gang so they executed him. Right away she had packed their things. "We are going north," she said. He had overheard his mother talking, "I don't know which is worse: to see my son forced to kill or being killed like my husband." It was a miracle they had made it across the border. Just as they crossed the finish line a patrol found him. His mother told him, "Don't worry. They will help us." They would ask for asylum and he could live with his aunt.

But he sat in a cage in a cold warehouse for two weeks, separated from his mother and placed with other children, who cried themselves to sleep at night. Many were sick. He barely ate the smelly food that seemed to give other kids the runs.

Weeks passed and slowly his tears stopped. He grew numb, his stomach hurt, and he could not eat the food. Suddenly the guards came and called his name. His mind raced with questions. *What will they do with me? Send me back? Move me to another prison?*

Then he saw her . . . his mother! They embraced and wept, his knees were weak, and she held him closer. He had no time to do more than look apologetically at the other children from the cell.

WHO STOLE MY BIBLE?

They were taken to an old yellow bus with wire on the windows. It dropped them at a nearby bus station. His mom was given a bag with documents and instructions that neither of them could read and a monitoring bracelet for her ankle. It looked like a shackle.

He stepped down warily from the bus and felt the warmth of the sun embrace him. Even the desert sun felt welcome after weeks in the warehouse, where the cold seemed to eat at his skin. There were some people who seemed to be waiting for them, although they do not know them. They look the boy in the eye, smile, and tell him to come. It felt strange to be seen.

He and the others from the bus followed them to a nearby house. Everyone was numb.

They came to a small building and saw even more Americans in front of the door. When they saw his group, they shouted, "Here they come!" Then, to the boy, they shouted: *"Bienvenidos!"* He felt like a hero, welcomed home from battle. He wondered why they were so happy to see him. He found himself smiling. He had forgotten what it was like to smile.

He was given chicken soup that tasted like his *abuela's*. Then a Sister brought him a big slice of birthday cake. *"Feliz Cumpleaños,"* she said with a wink, then ruffled his hair. It wasn't his birthday, but the cake was delicious.

His mother waited in the sitting area while a volunteer took him to play. His mother smiled and said, *"Está bien, no te preocupes. Son con la iglesia."* She said she would get directions to his aunt's home, and he watched as she plugged in the bracelet for her ankle.

As he played, a yellow-haired gringo, who said he was from New York City, asked what his dreams were for his life. He thought of the shouts of *"bienvenidos"* that greeted him and the people who gave him a meal. They were different from the guards who sometimes teased the children for crying.

He told the blond man: "I wish we were welcome here in America."

The guards talked about the new president who called them criminals. But these people here were kind. Maybe it could be different.

The boy headed out to the bus station with his mom. He felt like a new person now. It was more than the cake. The center was crowded, but there was so much . . . love. He looked back wondering what made them so kind and others so cruel. The sign over the door read, RESTORING HUMAN DIGNITY. He could not read those words, but he felt them.

A LESSON FOR US

The stories we find in Genesis are trying to "correct" the Mesopotamian accounts of creation and the flood that were circulating throughout the Near East at the time it was written. The biblical stories are designed to shape the moral consciousness of the ancient Israelites and refute the moral worldview of polytheistic traditions.[12]

Into a world where only the most ruthless and luckiest survive bursts a story about one God, who calls creation good, who creates human beings not from the blood of monsters, but in his own image. This God is moral. He hates violence and promises that no matter what hardship humans face, there will always be hope.

We long for a good god, but our human tendency is to make gods in our own image. Our view of God often reflects our flawed understanding of power and authority. Many of us grew up with a version of God as one who might smite us or send us to Hell. This is not the God of the creation story of Genesis. Many of our leaders embody the authoritarian gods of the Near East. They look for ways to control and exert their power over their followers. This is not the kind of community God desires.

One of the Psalms (115:8) describes well the connection between what kind of God we worship and how we live: "Those who make them (idols/gods) are like them, so are those who trust in them." What kind of God we follow has very much to do with our behavior in the world and the society we build together.

Authoritarian leaders are like the false, capricious gods that live according to their own selfish desires. Truth is what they say it is. They will belittle or even destroy others simply because they make too much noise like the humans in other creation stories. Cries for help, failure to fit in with social norms, expressed desires for justice—these are noise to tyrants and may warrant death or persecution. Tyrants do not want to hear the toddler crying, *"Mami, Papi!"* as prison guards make fun of her tears. They do not care for the trans person denied an apartment or a job, the family of a young Black man shot for wearing a hoodie, or the woman who speaks up about her abuse.

A tyrant poses as the defender of his people, but he takes away everyone's freedom, even from those who are of his tribe. The only course is to praise the tyrant and do what he says, or else. A tyrant takes away hope because there is no certainty that his anger will remain in check. A tyrant makes it feel as though he is a god, reigning for all eternity, and no other world order is possible.

But those who follow the God who calls creation good, who makes all in God's image, will make space for dignity to take root and for hope to flourish.

Using just a storefront in the quiet desert town of McAllen, Sister Norma Pimentel has done just that.

Modern Models: A Space for Dignity and Hope

Before Sister Norma became a nun with the Missionaries of Jesus, she hoped to become an artist. She studied fine arts in college and had plans to study architecture in graduate school, but then she recognized her calling to the Church. Sister Norma's God-given impulse to create beauty is manifested in her service to the immigrants and asylum seekers who come through the Rio Grande Valley. For over three decades, she has offered rest, comfort, food, and aid to countless migrants, first through the Casa Oscar Romero, then through Catholic Charities.

In 2014, Sister Norma opened the Humanitarian Respite Center to offer help to the unaccompanied minors arriving at the border. The vision for her center, posted above the door, is RESTORING HUMAN DIGNITY. The center she created reveals God's loving and merciful heart.

Sister Norma's witness to God's love-shaped politics has led her to weigh in on important political and policy issues. In 2019, when President Trump visited the Rio Grande Valley Sector, Sister Norma invited him to her center too. The president declined, choosing instead to try to co-opt her moral authority in a photo op to sanction his cruel policies on the border.[13] Yet, Sister Norma's hospitality and faithfulness in and of themselves are a rebuke of the false gods of power, authority, and political posturing. But it was also important that she use her voice to "image" God for the entire nation as her work became the center of national debates over how to treat migrant families.

In an opinion piece in the *Washington Post*, Sister Norma published an open letter to the president who came to her town, but failed to seek her out. She urged him to remember: "Regardless of who we are and where we came from, we remain part of the human family and are called to live in solidarity with one another."[14]

As Christians, we are all called to "image" God in every person. When we do this, we will find ourselves in opposition to leaders and systems that trample on human dignity rather than being co-opted by a tyrant or numbed to the cries of the vulnerable.

HOW WE RESIST
What can we do to strengthen this muscle? We can pray for those with whom we disagree. Pray for God to take hate or fear out of your heart. Pray for the well-being of those who anger or disturb you. Pray that, when speaking to those with whom you disagree,

you can be patient enough to hear what they are saying; then, with compassion, you can share your views. Congregations can pray together that they might hear one another well in these polarizing times. And we can provide opportunities to encounter "the other." Jim Henderson and his team are modeling this way of engaging with ideological opponents respectfully and peacefully through "The Three Practices." You can learn more about them here: www.3practices.com

It is critical to our spiritual development that we interact with a diversity of God's children. In our work at Faith in Public Life, we are building racially diverse multifaith networks in rural, as well as urban, areas. We don't all agree on every issue; but, by building trust and working together where we can, we have a starting place to image God not just in those we know, but in our towns, cities, and states as a whole.

Imaging God extends not just to our personal lives, but to our communal life, which includes our political life. Sometimes people see politics as "dirty" or distant from their matters of faithfulness and spiritual growth. Politics, according to Aristotle, who coined the term, simply means "matters of the city," or matters of our communal life. Human beings, Aristotle wrote, have a "perception of good and bad and right and wrong and the other moral qualities, and it is partnership in these things that makes a household and a city-state." Reflecting on Aristotle, my colleague Rabbi Seth Limmer explained: "Politics is the path, the art, or at least the term for the art, of how we share our moral sensibilities with our neighbors, express our understanding of what is right, and participate in the process of shaping our society."[15] We should advocate for policies that image God and for candidates that do a good job speaking and acting out of respect for all human beings.

Imaging God also means to ground our identity in God's love for all and guard against ideologies that might seduce us to protect our own kind. Some good questions to ask ourselves are: *Who do you belong to? God? Nation? Party? Your ethnic group or subculture? Whose are you?* If we follow the God in the Bible, we follow a God who loves all of humanity, not just one particular race or country. Our vision is bigger than our own nation's interests and certainly bigger than the interests of our class or ethnic group.

This is particularly critical to ponder as we live through an era in which our president is using the phrase "America First" to describe his policy agenda. We are Christians first, not Americans first. White nationalism is a belief system that puts loyalty, race, and nation at the center of a person's value system rather than biblical teachings about human dignity. White nationalism is antithetical to Christianity. In fact, many "alt-right" intellectuals hate Christianity for that very reason. One alt-right intellectual, Gregory Hood, has written that Christianity has inserted a "pathological altruism" into American culture. "Like acid," he wrote, "Christianity burns through the ties of kinship and blood" so critical to ethno-nationalist projects.[16]

Christian nationalism—a cultural framework that idealizes and advocates the fusion of Christianity with American civic life—is one of the strongest predictors of support for Trump say Andrew L. Whitehead and Samuel L. Perry in *Taking America Back for God: Christian Nationalism in the United States.* "The "Christianity" of Christian nationalism represents something more than religion—it includes assumptions about nativism, white supremacy, patriarchy, and heteronormativity along with divine sanction for authoritarian control and militarism."[17] Trump has laid extensive groundwork for his outward embrace of white nationalist agendas and Christian nationalism. We saw it when he called Mexicans rapists and African and Caribbean countries "s---hole countries"; when he refused to condemn Neo Nazi and KKK violence in Charlottesville; when he imposed a Muslim Ban; when he adopted policies that separated nursing babies and toddlers from their moms and dads and in his embrace of "religious freedom" as a fig leaf for discrimination against LGBTQ people.

WHO STOLE **MY BIBLE?**

By participating in God's compassionate care for humanity, people of faith can take a stand against the unjust and evil powers, principalities, and rulers who require allegiance at all costs. When people of faith choose the way of God, who, in Jesus, became both fully divine and fully human and declares that the last shall be first, they are resisting every tyrant who insists that the last shall be last. Genesis tells us we serve a God, who creates everyone in God's image. When we know this God, we are unable to tolerate or revere tyrants who rip children from their mothers' arms or fails to condemn white supremacy.

Discussion Questions

1. When you think of power and authority, what images come to mind?
2. How does the God of the Bible define and wield power and authority?
3. What kind of God did you grow up hearing about? Did you hear about the God who loved creation and humanity? The God who was defined by dominion over humanity?
4. How might individual or societal beliefs determine what type of governance and leadership people choose?

CHAPTER 3
Getting Off the Path to Autocracy

*This exodus God is different. . . . This God dœsn't need images
in the form of wood or stone or marble, because this God has
people. This God is looking for a body.*
—Rob Bell and Don Golden

Strong people don't need strong leaders.
—Ella Baker

Human beings were made in the image of God. At Sinai, the
Israelites were called to build a nation unlike any other—one
that followed a god who loves justice and hates the ways of
empires. However, God's people turned to idolatry. They built
a golden calf modeled on the gods of the region. Rather than
placing faith in a liberating god, who called them to build a society based on loving their neighbor, they submitted fearfully to
the gods of surrounding empires for protection.

Often we miss the depth of this idolatry. Yahweh was not
simply offended by their lack of loyalty, but by their failure to
embrace the new vision. Idolatry makes God over in the fashion
of empires. In making God over in the image of imperial de-
ities, the Israelites had voted to become like the other nations
rather than a nation built on an ethic of human dignity. They
rejected God's treaty with them, in particular, its ethical claims.
God's complaint (Exod. 32:8): "They have been quick to turn
aside from the way that I commanded them." In part, they have
violated the command not to make a likeness of God. But more

23

than that, they have turned away from *the way* or *the path* God showed them. To create a likeness of God that resembles the brutal gods of the region is to give themselves permission to stray from God's command to love their neighbor and welcome the stranger. Idolatry is the worship of that which leads us astray from God's liberative plan for humanity. The desire to act like the other nations—exploiting, dominating, excluding others—was idolatrous, and we find this running rampant in America and in our world today.

Our Past: Fearful, Faithless, and Fawning over a Golden Calf
My name is Shiphrah (Exod. 1:15–21) and I am with my people in the desert, having fled Egypt. One night, as we were waiting for guidance, our leaders decided to go their own way.

I drew closer to the men talking in urgent, hushed tones around the fire in an effort to hear what they were planning. I was one of the midwives who had saved so many babies from Pharaoh before we escaped from slavery.

They don't even see me, I thought. *But, no matter. God sees me.* I chuckled a little. *Being an invisible old woman has its advantages.*

I was close enough to hear them now. They were fearful. Moses was gone, gone to the mountain to talk with Yahweh. The men were looking fearfully through the flames at the distant mountaintop that was deepening to purple in the dying light. "Maybe he is dead," said one. "We need a backup plan," suggested another.

They are consumed with their fears, I realized, torn between anger and scorn. When will they ever learn? When we were in the desert, they grumbled about the food. God brought manna from Heaven and even provided enough on Friday for all so we could keep the Sabbath. Even so, some hoarded it in fear they would run out. Praise Yahweh's faithfulness!

Another time, when we ran out of water, God brought water from a rock. Over and over, God provided, and yet their fear had driven them to seek to put things under their own control. It never stopped! They grumbled; they hoarded; they bickered.

When God first spoke to my heart, my stomach churned as I reflected on Pharaoh's command to kill the sons of the Hebrews. I had prayed to the God of Joseph and found courage. Puah (rest her soul) and I had spread the word to the midwives of the kingdom. "Resist," we whispered. "God will provide."

That was when I met Miriam, Moses' sister. Miriam stood straight and tall, her long, dark hair flowing down her back. She looked people in the eyes, and her own burned like fire. She had a deep, clear singing voice.

Miriam organized the families. It was Miriam who thought to build life rafts from reeds. "Pretend to comply, but float them to safety, like this," she whispered to pregnant women as she made gentle pushing motions with her capable hands.

Miriam knew Bityah, Pharaoh's daughter, from childhood. They had met as young girls when Miriam strayed from home and wandered into the palace bathing area. Miriam was bold even as a child.

Bityah rescued as many Hebrew babies as she could from her father's butchery, working with other Egyptian women. When another child was placed in a basket, Miriam would sing a liberation song so that Bityah, waiting on the other side of the river, knew it was time to keep watch.

We women stuck together and saved hundreds of infants. Even when the guards came, even when they took Puah, we never lost hope. Never. And now we were free!

The lightning cracked, and my mind returned to my immediate surroundings. The men jumped, and one shouted, "Damn it to Hell! I wish we were still in Egypt! At least we knew what the next day would bring!"

Aaron spoke up, nervous at the growing restlessness of the crowd. "We will make a golden calf and pray to it for safety." Aaron was always looking to keep people busy rather than inspire them.

He looked around the crowd and saw the men's faces relax. His idea landed well. "Go, gather the gold smuggled out of Egypt. We will melt it down to make a calf."

The bull god of military might! We worship Yahweh, the God who dismantles empires.

Suddenly the lightning lit the sky as brightly as day for an instant. I looked up and met Aaron's eyes. He shrugged when he saw my critical gaze as if to suggest: "What else can I do?"

I stared back until Aaron looked away.

If only Miriam were in charge.

UNDERSTANDING THE TEXT

Having endured the trauma of slavery, the danger of a daring rebellion and a perilous escape, the Israelites arrived at Mount Sinai. There, God would enter into a direct covenant with God's liberated people.

This story is known as "The Ten Commandments," but the title seems too puny to cover the moment described in Exodus 19. Too often, the Ten Commandments conjure up the image of a list of do's and don'ts carrying dire ramifications to anyone who transgresses against them. God offered the Israelites more than a book of rules. Here on Sinai, the God who brought the Israelites out from slavery was inviting them into a new way of living together as a people. Having fled a brutal empire, they were charged with the task of building, with God's help, an alternative to imperial ways. They would build a nation based not on domination and exploitation, but on love of neighbor and human dignity. Many of us picture the delivery of the Ten Commandments in Exodus as a single, dramatic event (á la Cecil B. DeMille), but the law was given over a period of forty years and spans the books of Exodus, Numbers, Deuteronomy, and Leviticus.

The Sinai or Mosaic covenant follows the format of ancient Near East treaties between Emperors and their lesser kings. The Sinai "treaty" was radically unique in that God is the law creator, not an earthly ruler. No other case exists in the ancient world of a god giving the people its law.

Also unique is the fact that God's laws were the responsibility of all the Israelites, not just Moses. Israel was to be a "nation of priests" (Exod. 19:5b). Each person, regardless of their station in life, was charged with the responsibility of living by these guide-stones that would show them the way to draw closer to God. The whole community would be blessed if they followed the law, cursed if they did not. The natural result of listening to God's charge was blessing. The natural outcome of ignoring God's signposts was misery.

This was a stark divergence from what they knew. In ancient times, the law was issued by the king and punitive only: no blessings, only threats. Obey me or die. Not so with the Sinai treaty. The law was to be brought before the entire people (Exod. 21:1) and read to them so they could learn God's ways and enter into a direct relationship as priests of a holy nation. Parents were told to educate their children to live in these ways (Deut. 6:6–7). The fact that God makes this treaty with everyone is a democratizing act in and of itself.

Israel was not only to be a nation of priests, but a holy nation (Exod. 19:5b). The word "holy" means "designated." Designated for what? Designated for a unique role among other nations that are also God's. If they keep God's covenant or treaty, they will be God's people. But then there is this verse: "Indeed the whole earth is mine, but you shall be for me a priestly kingdom." God's vision is larger than one nation or people, although Israel has a special charge. God's interest is all of humanity. If we take this moment at Sinai to be the purist glimpse at who God is, unfiltered by human misunderstanding and some of the problematic chapters of the Bible, then it is clear that here God rejects nationalism. Although Israel is a special people, all creation is loved by God, and God has a plan for all creation.

To summarize, in these first utterances at Sinai we learn immediately that God—not a king—is the powerful author of all goodness. All Isra-elites are charged with advancing this goodness and being a model for other nations. These, in and of themselves, are democratizing revelations. The system of domination common in most societies and certainly among the empires of the ancient Near East is being dissolved at the highest level—with God.

WHO STOLE **MY BIBLE?**

Both in Exodus 19:4 and Exodus 20:2, God self-identifies as "the LORD your God who brought you out of the land of Egypt; out of the house of slavery."

This self-descriptor is one of the most common descriptors of God in the first five books of the Bible. Scripture refers to God way more often as "the God who brought you out of Egypt" (thirty-two times) than it does to God as "Creator" (six times).[1]

The centrality of this verse is often lost on Christians today, but some translations of the Bible gave it its rightful place. Martin Luther's translation of the Bible into German calls Genesis "I Moses," in other words, "The First Book of Moses." Hence, "In the beginning" is a story first told to liberated slaves. A number of scholars argue that the Book of Exodus is the first book of the Bible. Having explored the creation story, we can see how the story synchronizes perfectly with the Exodus journey and the Mosaic Covenant.[2]

Christian prayers often start with the words "Creator God," yet seldom with "Liberating God." However, to pray to our Creator is to pray to the God who hates slavery, whose laws give us direction for building communities that eliminate oppression.

The First Command (second in Judaism) says, "You shall have no other gods before me." It is this command that they violate when building an idol. Some say the statue resembled Baal, the Canaanite bull god, who represented military might and fertility. Others say it was the goddess Hathor of Egypt— the goddess that Yahweh defeated in order to lead them out of slavery. There are at least two possibilities here: One is that they turned to worshiping a more militaristic, imperial god, rejecting the vision of following the God who liberates. Second is that they built an idol to offer blood sacrifices in an effort to placate and control Yahweh, whose nearby presence terrified them.

Either way, idolatry clearly has much to do with deviating from trust in God the Liberator and freer of slaves. The first step in the downward spiral is forgetting who God is. Catholic theologian Rosemary Radford Ruether says that idolatry is the setting up of certain human figures as the privileged images and representations of God. In her work addressing erroneous theologies that oppress women, she writes: "To the extent that such political and ecclesiastical patriarchy incarnates unjust and oppressive relationships, such images of God become sanctions of evil."[3] Through the revelation of God in the burning bush to Moses, God conveys that God cannot be reduced or controlled. God's name is "I am what I shall be," a word without vowels, that cannot be pronounced by humans.

Other theologians point to the motivation that leads people to take their focus off God. Brazilian educator and activist Paulo Freire in *Pedagogy of the Oppressed* wrote that idolatry and oppression go hand in hand because both are about control— the effort to control God and people.[4] Martin Buber, the German theologian who witnessed the devastating effect of widespread dehumanization under the Nazi regime, wrote of idolatry as the treatment of people as things.[5] Rather than placing the image of God in people, as the Bible tells us to do, people begin to deify material wealth, power, control. Rabbi Nahum Ward-Lev observes that the prophets saw that idolatry and injustice are co-occurring. He writes that the prophets "saw that controlling people through oppressive systems and attempting to control God through idolatrous practices go hand in hand."[6] There are those who will seek to image God in such a way as to control and abuse others. But why do those with the most to lose often fall for this? After all God has offered us, why do we succumb to idolatry?

As a child, my first reaction to this story was judgment and disbelief. As the oldest girl among five children, so I carried parental responsibility early in life, I identified with poor Moses. He came home to a royal mess. The text says the people were "running wild" (Exod. 32:25). In Exodus 32:17–18, loyal Joshua reported this scene to Moses: "There is a noise of war in the camp. But it is not the sound made by victors, or the sound made by losers; it is the sound of revelers that I hear."

The scene is demoralizing and shocking. As an adult, I am coming to understand better how this could happen. The road to following a liberative God requires determination, resilience, and utter trust in God's ways, despite one's impossible circumstances. Rabbi Ward-Lev suggests that the emotional anguish of slavery had crushed their spirit. God does not offer us an escape from hardship. The path to liberation is full of unknowns, of terrifying moments, and of outright failures. To study any movement in depth is to realize that the way forward was anything but clear and certain. For the Israelites, it was difficult to perceive, despite all the miracles they witnessed, that a way forward without empire was possible.[7]

This is the task before all of us. Do we trust in God's charge at Sinai that a new way of living together is possible even when things are going south? Or will we turn to forms of religion or ideologies that seek to control God and others?

America Today: Financing False Gods and Gospels

The idolatry at Sinai is not that far from many of our experiences today. The culture we live and breathe can often be stronger than we know, teaching us to worship a false god or attempt to control God and others.

Some of us have grown up hearing a fire-and-brimstone gospel that depicts a god waiting to jump on our misdeeds. We were taught to live in fear of God and with deep shame about who we are. We've heard sermons all of our lives about what will befall us if we have sex outside marriage, if we are LGBTQ, if we drink alcohol or do drugs. This is a wrathful god who sharply watches us to ensure we comply with a list of pietistic dos and don'ts that often have little to do with scripture. This image of God, drilled into our heads at an early age, makes it difficult to imagine a god who loves us and wants to show us how to live in love and justice for all.

If hellfire sermons weren't drummed into you, prosperity gospel may have been the message you heard. Prosperity gospel teaches that if we do all the right things (including making a sizable donation), God will make us healthy and wealthy. The converse to that is that if we do not do what God wants, we might get cancer or we will struggle with financial hardship. Prosperity gospel teaches that the sick and marginalized have brought calamity on themselves, and if they will get right with God, all will be well. One need only look at the lives of the prophets and Jesus to know that God's purpose with us does not involve wealth or an easy life, but following God does bring us closer to love and joy, which is far greater than simple happiness. God is not a magic genie or slot machine, where you put in your wish or your coins and you get your material reward. God cannot be controlled by our donations or actions. Prosperity gospel is syncretistic in that it has melded religion with the surrounding culture of consumerism and hypercapitalism, which wants us to believe human beings can be valued by their net worth.

A third false gospel is the country club gospel. We go to church to look like upstanding citizens, learn a bit, drop our kids at Sunday school to learn how to be decent human beings. We network. We glad-hand. We strike deals. But there is little in the way of instruction for how to follow the God who charges us with creating a just society. We donate to missions, but we leave unexamined the systems that comfort us while grinding our poorer neighbors into dust.

But it gets worse. Historically, the Bible has been used for causes antithetical to God's purposes. Christianity has been used to advance tyranny rather than undo it. American slaveholders created a slaveholder Christianity full of biblical justifications for the brutal treatment of enslaved people of African ancestry. Apartheid South Africa closely paralleled the arguments used by white Christian slaveholders. Nazi Germany took over the German Church within months, and the majority of theologians and clergy bowed to Hitler as he spoke of himself as a god clearly intent on genocide. All of these ideologies were rooted in a version of Christianity that cast God as white. God has been imaged as male as well, and women being cast as inferior to men results in the abuse—physically, economically, spiritually—of women and girls.

God was melted down and recast in the image of the very genocidal tyrants the Yahweh of the Bible sought to cast down. This is the height of idolatry. People are still dying from the aftershocks. America is still fighting the war against slavery and the economic apartheid that followed as Black, Brown, and indigenous people are targeted with surgical precision by voter suppression laws, criminal justice systems bent on subjugation, deportation mechanisms, and white supremacist violence. Women are still struggling for equal representation, the right to live free from violence, and economic equality with men.

Authoritarians design a punishing god. Those who worship wealth design an ATM god. Press the right buttons and you will get everything you ever wanted. Pay to play. The lord of the manor holds fantastic parties for the blessed and comfortable. Those who want to rule as tyrants make God over to be a tyrant. A white supremacist. A strongman.

God promised us the stars. But some who seek control, rather than freedom, constantly reduce God to an empty vessel of a bull. Even more horrific, some reduced God to Auschwitz, Robben Island, and the lynching tree.

A LESSON FOR US

In recent days, I have seen a disturbing picture of our current president, one unlike any I've seen before. In a well-publicized photograph, President Trump surrounds himself with religious leaders who show him unquestioning loyalty. Their heads are bowed in prayer, their eyes closed. The president stands in the center towering over them, making them look submissive, obsequious. His arms are folded. He looks straight at the camera. The pose of a strongman. The backdrop is black—taken in a studio. It's clear the photo was staged very carefully; it is not a live shot. The photo is designed to send a message.

Trump is being worshiped. The picture makes it clear that he does not need to pray. As he said during his campaign, he has no need to repent. He is perfect. As he has famously said: "Only I can fix this." Not, "Together we can build another nation." Trump is suggesting he is above the need to repent or to pray—perhaps he himself is a god, or, at the very least, God's anointed. His supporters have suggested as much. In an interview on the Christian Broadcasting Network (CBN) on January 30, 2019, with CBN's political analyst David Brody and senior Washington correspondent Jennifer Wishon, Sarah Huckabee Sanders, Trump's press secretary, said, "I think God calls all of us to fill different roles at different times, and I think that he wanted Donald Trump to become president." Pastor Robert

Jeffress, a Texas Baptist and prominent Trump supporter, has promoted the idea that Trump holds office due to divine intervention. "Millions of Americans believe the election of President Trump represented God giving us another chance—perhaps our last chance—to truly make America great again."[8] The tyrant is a god. God has been made over in the fashion of a tyrant. This is idolatry.

On December 19, 2019, Mark Galli, the editor of the flagship evangelical magazine *Christianity Today*, wrote an editorial titled "Trump Should Be Removed from Office." Evidence made it clear that Trump attempted to use his official power to coerce a foreign leader to harass and dishonestly discredit one of the president's political opponents. Galli referenced Sinai: "That he should be removed, we believe, is not a matter of partisan loyalties but loyalty to the Creator of the Ten Commandments. To the many evangelicals who continue to support Mr. Trump in spite of his blackened moral record, we might say this: Remember who you are and whom you serve."[9]

The call to remember who you are and whom you serve is the spiritual discipline that enables us all to follow our conscience rather than commit idolatry by giving unquestioning loyalty to an authoritarian.

Six weeks later, as the Senate voted on impeachment, only one Republican stood firm. Mitt Romney, a member of the Church of Jesus Christ of Latter-day Saints (Mormon Church), stood before the nation and uttered these emotional words:

> "But my promise before God to apply impartial justice required that I put my personal feelings and political biases aside. Were I to ignore the evidence that has been presented, and disregard what I believe my oath and the Constitution demands of me for the sake of a partisan end, it would, I fear, expose my character to history's rebuke and the censure of my own conscience."

Mitt Romney and Mark Galli have been attacked and marginalized by Trump. It is not easy to go against the grain. Yes, you can lose your community, some of your family and friends, even your livelihood. But the prophets were imprisoned, ostracized, tossed out into exile, hunted, sometimes killed.

Consider the alternative: worshiping a strongman does not end well for anyone.

Modern Models: Speaking Truth to Power

My friend James Salt reminds me of the prophets of Hebrew Scripture. He is fearless and grounded in a vision of justice. Once, he confronted Rep. Paul Ryan with a Bible to ask him if he would read the Gospel of Luke to his legislative staff rather than ask them to read Ayn Rand, the libertarian, Jesus-hating philosopher who advocated for a survival-of-the-fittest economy. We happened to videotape the encounter, and it went viral, making its way even into the pages of the *Wall Street Journal*.

In early October 2011, I found myself building a golden calf in James's basement. He had a picture of the Wall Street bull statue up on his computer screen. He had rolls of chicken wire collected from a nearby dump. He had mixed some papier-mâché. As we went to work, I felt giddy with excitement. We had found a way to add our moral witness to the Occupy Wall Street cause at Zuccotti Park in Manhattan.

On September 17, 2011, a group of young protesters had taken over Zuccotti Park. They were there to protest corporate influence on democracy, the lack of legal consequences for those who brought about the global financial crisis, and an immoral inequality of wealth between the wealthiest 1 percent and the rest of us. Congress had bailed out Wall Street banks, which had irresponsibly crashed the global economy by creating a massive housing bubble that ultimately burst. While banks got bailed out, the average American paid the price.

Having almost bought a house before this collapse, I understood how it happened. I stood in front of the real estate agent with our fidgety one-year-old boy on my hip and my husband beside me. I told our agent that we had decided we would have to rent rather than buy. With bids escalating to $100,000 over asking price, we found we could not compete. The banks had cleared us for more money than I thought we could ever pay off. It was too risky.

The agent looked me in the eye and said, "You will be shut out forever." He was telling me in no uncertain terms that I had failed my family. Two years later, the market collapsed and many lost everything. Did I feel vindicated? No. Many of my friends were hurt, and I have yet to realize my dream of owning a home. Homes remain overvalued because of a corrupt, abusive banking system. Those at the top made out well. Those of us at the bottom, and in the middle, continue to struggle with the costs of living.

For me, this cause was as personal as it was moral. The world needed a new vision for who we could be. The golden calf was our way to convey that vision.

Even so, James and I and a few other friends had debated whether or not our golden calf would send a clear message. Some thought the reference was too obscure. They argued no one would make the connection to Sinai, idolatry, and greed. Could the power of our biblical beliefs break through and move the public debate?

Any sliver of doubt evaporated that Saturday evening as I helped James unload the idolatrous calf from a van parked on Bleecker Street in the West Village, a street lined with music clubs and bars, and close to the New York University campus and famous Washington Square Park. We carried the golden calf to Judson Memorial Church for its overnight resting place.

It was New York, so we didn't think anyone would blink at the sight of an odd object moving precariously down the sidewalk. But right away, we heard a college student hanging out a bar window shout, "Dude! A golden calf of greed! Right on!" I knew then that we'd done a fantastic job of blending the images in children's picture Bibles with the famous Wall Street bull statue. For good measure, when we got to the church near Zuccotti Park, I asked that we paint "greed" on the front side of the base and "idolatry" on the side.

The next morning, Rev. Donna Schaper at Judson Memorial Church in the Village preached on the golden calf. As God would have it, Exodus 32 was the lectionary text that day! That was just a godly coincidence, not strategic planning. After Rev. Schaper's sermon—a perfect blend of pastoral care and prophetic imagination—the congregants marched the calf two miles down Broadway to Zuccotti Park. The volunteer calf bearers were dressed as Wall Street bankers, wearing dark black suits, crisp ties, and sleek dark sunglasses. By the time we reached the park, we had hundreds of people joining the marching in support of our moral critique. Reporters and news cameras tracked our movements. The drums of protest grew louder as we drew near our destination, and I felt that we were indeed back at Sinai.

The pictures of the golden calf at Occupy Wall Street went viral, running alongside AP stories nationwide and even appearing on the cover of the *New York Review of Books*, sparking moral debates across the country and the world.

Soon after our golden calf march, Pope Francis wrote how inequality kills in *Evangelii Gaudium* (*The Joy of the Gospel*). In this treatise on the future of the church and spreading the Gospel, the pope spoke beautifully of how the root of the Gospel is liberation and justice. Evangelism must advocate for a market that brings life rather than death to God's children—all of us.

The debate continued through the 2012 election season as my friend Sister Simone Campbell led the Nuns on the Bus tour around the country to challenge an economy based on greed. As Catholics, they challenged Rep. Paul Ryan, the Catholic vice-presidential candidate, on his proposals to cut social safety net programs while cutting taxes for the wealthiest 1 percent. That year, moral outrage over greed and the hoarding of wealth by the rich and powerful, while millions struggled to provide for their families, became a top election issue.

In the final years of the Obama administration, the third President's Advisory Council on Faith-based and Neighborhood Partnerships was charged with tackling economic equality. I was appointed to chair the council. I was grateful that the administration invited faith leaders to not only talk about poverty, but also to look into the drivers behind economic inequality unparalleled since the 1920s.

We were religiously diverse and from constituencies that voted with both parties. Representatives of the Salvation Army, Covenant House, a Catholic University of America think tank, and National Latino Evangelical Coalition sat alongside community organizers, Black Lives Matter supporters, Sikhs, Muslims, and the first trans woman to serve on the council.

Our job was not to praise the president, but to challenge him. Our recommendations tackled racial equity and the global dimensions of inequality. We demanded the administration do more to address implicit bias in the criminal justice system, including mass incarceration and police brutality that stripped resources from communities of color. We called for the administration to end the incarceration of immigrant children, to back the Standing Rock Sioux as they protested the Dakota Access Pipeline, and to curb deportations.

We wrestled. We pushed back when necessary. Our efforts paid off. Power concedes nothing without a demand. Our role as faith leaders is to challenge, not blindly follow those in office, even those we admire.

HOW WE RESIST
These moments have taught me that the ability to confront leaders—even those we support—who fail to image God in every person is a critical spiritual discipline. Often we are conditioned

to believe that being faithful demands complete loyalty—even to the point of blind obedience—to those in power. Many of our institutions establish strict hierarchies and discourage any debate or questions. Pastors who commit sexual misconduct or abuse power in other ways go unchallenged. Politicians from our own party are not held accountable. The story of the golden calf challenges us to ask again whose we are; to scrutinize whether or not we are listening to God and speaking out when our conscience, shaped by the Holy Spirit and Scripture, alerts us that something is wrong. In these moments, it is critical to meditate on this: Whom do we belong to? The God who liberates slaves and advances human dignity or the God who advances our personal power and calms our fears? Such questions can keep us grounded and help us to discuss our concerns with both those who lead and with our community.

I learned in these moments that it is critical for our nation and the world that we call out idolatry publicly, especially that which originates from those who speak from our faith tradition. In the case of the golden calf, our symbolic act of carrying a visual critique of Wall Street's idolatry in solidarity with Occupy Wall Street prompted a critical debate. Sister Simone Campbell and Nuns on the Bus accomplished the same goals. Challenging a president whom the faith community admired and supported was also a critical lesson in how to live out biblical teachings. In a world of tyrants, one sign that you are being faithful to God is that you are challenging those who hold worldly power.

Last, it is critical that we internalize that following God does not always result in material reward or happiness as the world gives. The future may look bleak at times. We may find it looks as though there is no way forward. At times we may despair. We will be tempted perhaps to turn to a leader who can save us. But God tells us there is no one alone who can fix it. We are the ones we have been waiting for. Together we must fix it. We are not after a material reward, but rather a spiritual one—the joy that God gives as we struggle alongside God for the liberation of humanity from all oppression. God never promised wealth. God promised we would know love and life abundantly. In this, there is freedom and liberation from all that binds us: our fears, our addictions, our insecurities, our chains.

Discussion Questions

1. Do you agree with the author's definition of idolatry as the worship of that which leads us astray from God's liberative plan for humanity? Why?
2. Where do you see idolatry today? What is the result of that idolatry?
3. What are ways to counter idolatrous behavior? Does going against the grain feel like a spiritual discipline? Why?

CHAPTER 4
Remembering What We Came From

History is collapsing on itself once again.
—Austin Channing Brown

For generations after their liberation from slavery and God's offer of the Mosaic covenant at Sinai, the Israelites were a "nation of priests" inspired by prophets and judges. They had no king. Sinai created a system of government run more by and for the people. But the people struggled mightily from the start, as we saw with the golden calf story. The prophet Samuel had led them faithfully, but his sons were corrupt (1 Sam. 8:1-3). They took bribes and perverted justice. The Philistine threat loomed large.

As threats loomed, rather than double down on God's system for securing justice for all, the people begged Samuel for a king.

The Israelites' demand for a king is a warning left by the authors of these holy texts—our spiritual ancestors. God offers freedom and liberation; yet in fear and frustration, we choose the ways of the world. We choose to be ruled rather than govern ourselves; we choose the devil we know rather than God's new thing.

Our Past: We Want a King!
Picture God and Samuel sitting together on the front stoop,

talking about a problem, like parents discussing their child's behavior. Samuel, sad faced, turns to God and says, "Somehow I failed you." (I Samuel 8:7)

God looks far away and sighs, "No, no, it's not on you. It's me. It's me they don't get. They don't want me, the God of liberation, to be their king. They want to be like Egypt and Babylon. They have forgotten they were once slaves and it was I, Yahweh, that brought them out."

God and I sat there on the stoop for a few minutes, crestfallen.

God thought for a minute and then looked at me, seemingly totally defeated. "They have not rejected you. They have rejected me," God said gently.

Again we sat in silence, contemplating this new and daunting spiritual impasse.

Then God sighed deeply and exhaled slowly in resignation. "So, here's what we do. Let them have a king."

I looked at God, stunned.

"But warn them," God said, looking sadly into the distance. "Let them know what will unfold."

I did as God said:

> *This is what the king who will reign over you will claim as his rights:*
>
> *He will take your sons and make them serve with his chariots and horses, and they will run in front of his chariots. Some he will assign to be commanders of thousands and commanders of fifties, and others to plow his ground and reap his harvest, and still others to make weapons of war and equipment for his chariots.*
>
> *He will take your daughters to be perfumers and cooks and bakers. He will take the best of your fields and vineyards and olive groves and give them to his attendants.*

> *He will take a tenth of your grain and of*
> *your vintage and give it to his officials and*
> *attendants. Your male and female servants and*
> *the best of your cattle[c] and donkeys he will*
> *take for his own use.*
>
> *He will take a tenth of your flocks, and you*
> *yourselves will become his slaves.* (I Samuel 8:1-
> 7)

UNDERSTANDING THE TEXT

Six times, the phrase "He will take" is used in God's warning.

The king will take from the people, until one day: "You yourselves will become his slaves." If this were a movie, we would hear thunder rumbling in the background or see a shadow fall over their faces.

Note this list of takings. You will see this again as we move to the next chapter. What do kings do? They design an economic system that exploits everyone's labor for the king and the king's circle. Wealth becomes concentrated in the hands of a privileged few. It becomes harder for the people to support themselves as their labor is exploited by those who hoard resources. The king builds an army, becoming more and more aggressive. The vast resources of the people increasingly go into militarizing everything. Soon people are impoverished and dominated by a police state and a permanent state of war. They become slaves to the king's ambitions.

These words, this warning, mark the beginning of the era of kings. Samuel anoints Saul. King Saul goes mad. Samuel anoints King David. David abuses his power by murdering a man and stealing his wife. The prophet Nathan confronts him. David repents, and God forgives him. But his sins are visited on his sons, who are quite a mess. When David dies, Solomon assumes the throne. Solomon is so oppressive that after he dies, a civil war breaks out. The kingdom divides.

The Mosaic covenant had laid out a legal framework that

repudiated slavery, welcomed foreigners and refugees, provided for the poor, and prevented entrenched inequality. Some tenets of the Law of Moses, like the ideal of jubilee debt relief, were more radical in many ways than our own democracy.

The exhortation and invitation to be a nation of priests—one in which everyone could lead by upholding the ethic of loving your neighbor—had the potential to become the cornerstone of a new leadership structure for creating a new world. Why did the people reject it?

Having been rescued from the brutality of Pharaoh, the Israelites soon found themselves in need of deliverance from the pitiless Canaanite rulers who had ensnared and subjugated them. From the twelfth to the eleventh centuries BCE, "there was no king in Israel." In times of trouble, God appointed judges to lead them, but God was their king. Repeatedly they also fell short of the covenant's demands and God called them to repent. By the time they approached Samuel to ask for a king, they were up against a Philistine threat and divided internally by greed and corruption. Samuel's sons, who were expected to lead when he died, had failed God's vision by taking bribes, and perverting justice all for their own personal gain (I Sam. 8:3b).

Terrified by threats of invasion and unable to implement the covenant's demands around equality and justice, they rejected God's proposal to be a society where political authority resides in the hands of the people. In a moment of desperation, the old ways looked more promising than the new.

"By the eighth century BCE, a time of prosperity in Israel and Judah, the disparity between the rich and the poor had become extreme," writes Rabbi Nahum Ward-Lev.[1] The society that had embraced God's liberating vision for the world was headed down the road to autocracy.

America Today: We Got a King, Not a President

The Bible teaches us that there is something about human nature that loves a king, that rejects shared power. In times of fear and instability, people tend to choose a strongman over and against this vision of being a nation of priests charged with implementing an ethical vision of governance. Today we use words like "democracy" to describe a government that is by and for the people, a government that protects minority rights and free speech. The opposite of democracy is a government in which power is concentrated in the hands of a few, a government that does not allow freedoms of speech, press, and religion or protect minority rights.

Growing up, I never thought I would live to see a day where American democracy was gravely threatened from within. I knew that we had, at best, been a deeply flawed democracy, having systematically excluded people of color, women, LGBTQ people, and religious minorities from the benefits of our so-called democracy. But I thought we were ever on the path to becoming a full democracy. Democratic backsliding happened in other countries, not here in America.

Prior to the 2016 election, Freedom House and the Economist Intelligence Unit, two organizations that publish scorecards on the strength of democracies around the world, both downgraded the United States from "democracy" to "flawed democracy" status. Economic inequality, wealth concentrated in white communities, erosion of voting rights, mass incarceration, increased school segregation, and the influence of big money in politics were among some of the data points they used to support their position.

We are not alone. Authoritarianism is rising throughout the world. Hungary and Poland now have autocratic leaders. Right-wing authoritarians in 2017 gained votes and parliamentary seats in France, Netherlands, Austria, and Germany, and their success weakened parties on the right and the left. Ukraine's application to join the European Union in 2014 was interrupted by a Russian cyber campaign to elect a president sympathetic to Russia and a Russian invasion of Crimea.

I always thought of democracies as dying dramatic deaths.

In the nineties, I led a Presbyterian Peacemaking Program delegation to Argentina and Chile to learn about the role church leaders and theologians played in advancing democracy under horribly oppressive regimes. When I thought of democracies ending, I always pictured the military rolling through the streets and generals issuing decrees from the South Lawn at the White House. And we have seen some tanks in the streets—Ferguson, DC, and Portland, for example. We have seen a general walk across Lafayette Park to St. John's Church after teargassing peaceful protesters.

But, political scientists say, for the most part, democracies are dying slow, quiet deaths these days. They "erode slowly, in barely visible steps," according to Steven Levitsky and Daniel Ziblatt in *How Democracies Die.*[2] "Blatant dictatorship—in the form of fascism, communism, or military rule—has disappeared across much of the world."[3] Most authoritarian countries even hold regular elections. Because there is no single moment— no coup or suspension of the constitution—nothing may set off society's alarm bells. Those who announce the erosion of democratic norms may even be dismissed as exaggerating.

A LESSON FOR US

The authoritarian leaders of this era take four steps to concentrate their power.[4]

First, they reject the democratic rules of the game, often by subtle methods like canceling or undermining the legitimacy of elections through redistricting, voter suppression, banning opposition organizations, closing polling places, "losing" ballots, and restricting civil rights.

Second, authoritarians deny the legitimacy of political opponents. In more extreme situations, they jail or assassinate their opponents.

But today's autocrats might merely threaten to jail political opponents based on vague, unproven accusations ("Lock her up!"). They use tactics such as firing or shunning those in government who speak out against corruption to make it clear that nothing but total acquiescence will be tolerated. Without the cornerstone of debate, dissent, and compromise, democracies slowly fail.

Third, authoritarians encourage violence.

More dramatic versions of authoritarianism might capitalize on ties to police, paramilitary groups, guerrillas, or armed guards. They might simply endorse violence by refusing to clearly condemn it, or even by expressing admiration for it. Or they might fan the flames of violence with tweets like "Liberate Michigan!" or the segregationist slogan: "When the looting starts, the shooting starts."

Last, an authoritarian leader shows readiness to curtail civil liberties of opponents, including journalists.

They might jail, harass, or assassinate, or they might simply demonize them as "the enemy of the people" in retaliation against critical coverage. Rather than respond or address factual news reports, authoritarian leaders marginalize the news as fake. In the eighties, we feared the type of state-controlled media described in George Orwell's *1984*, which depicted what was happening in the Soviet Union. Today propaganda comes from corporate-run entertainment news masquerading as news, when it is, in fact, disinformation. It is easy to produce fake news. No one has a shared reality or truth. Without shared facts, it is difficult to debate and build consensus for decision making.

Understanding these four steps that authoritarians use to concentrate power can be helpful in our analysis of the spiritual sickness creeping through our society and political system. Addressing this brokenness requires a biblical and theological analysis and prayer. If those are done, we will find ourselves propelled to act courageously even in the face of great danger or, for those of us privileged by race, class, sexuality, or gender, the loss of a certain amount of safety and privilege.

The warning in I Samuel 8 closely parallels modern definitions of autocracy. God warns the Israelites that kings channel resources toward militarization and concentrate resources in the hands of a select few—while making things economically impossible for the majority.

Studying history is a critical spiritual discipline to guard against the human tendency to embrace authoritarian rule. I know this was not everyone's favorite subject in school. But when history is approached truthfully and passionately, and as a spiritual discipline, it can energize us to take charge of our own destiny.

Unfortunately, we are often taught a whitewashed version of history. Rarely did any of my classes relate history to current events, which would help demonstrate the relevance. Textbooks, even in the United States, have often politicized, and therefore censored, certain inconvenient truths from our history.[5] For decades after the Civil War, the Daughters of the Confederacy dedicated themselves to rewriting American history to advance the South's claims about the benevolence of slavery. Americans in particular receive a version of history that assumes our history is progressive—that our democracy and our society are getting increasingly enlightened each decade.

This largely American penchant for believing history always progresses is what historian Timothy Snyder calls a "politics of inevitability."[6] This can lead us to assume that our lives and our democracy will continue to improve naturally, without excessive vigilance and commitment. It causes us to believe democracy is improving, even though it is actually regressing. Sadly, it results in a failure to see our agency—that what we do or don't do determines where history goes.

The election of a president who appointed white supremacists to his cabinet led many Americans—particularly those of us who are white and therefore out of touch with the realities of people of color—to question our assumptions about American democracy, as did the racial justice protests after the murder of George Floyd in Minneapolis. It woke many of us up to a reality that we should have been alerted to long ago. As one racial justice advocate lamented, "That's what we've been trying to tell y'all!"

Prophetic religious leaders, such as Rev. William Barber, are lifting up a vision for our future by helping us better understand our white supremacist history.

Modern Models: Revolutionary Love

It was 7:00 a.m., the day after the 2016 election, and Jonathan Wilson-Hartgrove, a white evangelical writer and organizer, received a phone call from his friend the Rev. William Barber II. Rev. Barber said he had spent the wee hours of the morning poring over First Samuel. He was studying the passage we explored above, where God tells Samuel, "They have not rejected you, but they have rejected me."[7]

The nation had just elected Donald J. Trump. Everyone was shocked. But to Rev. Barber, this looked familiar. He had been fighting racist attacks on democracy in his home state of North Carolina and had seen other states succumbing to the same antidemocratic virus. While many of us were slumbering, North Carolina had faced a very similar playbook that the rest of the nation was now witnessing. Barber reportedly told Jonathan that morning: "America is North Carolina now."[8]

What did he mean by that? In 2012, North Carolina experienced a political shock. Despite its reputation as a moderate state compared to its Southern neighbors, hard-right Republicans swept the 2012 election and took control of the governorship and legislature, stunning political analysts who had seen Barack Obama win the state in 2008. Within months, the legislature pushed one of the most conservative agendas in the country. It passed restrictive voter ID laws that "targeted African-American voters with almost surgical precision," as a federal court ruling years later announced.[9] They blocked Medicaid coverage to as many as 500,000 people. Close analysis revealed that the victory had been fueled by cash from groups backed by the Koch brothers and other very wealthy donors, such as North

Carolina's Art Pope, enabling the Republican Party to win the governor's mansion and the state legislature in the same year for the first time since the Reconstruction era.[10]

As head of the North Carolina NAACP, Rev. Barber had already assembled a coalition called Historic Thousands on Jones Street (HkonJ) in 2007. Months after the hard-right takeover of North Carolina in 2012, Barber held a press conference at Davie Street Presbyterian Church in Raleigh, just a few blocks from the capitol building. There he proclaimed, "There must be a witness in the face of extremism and regressive public policy." Calling up the strategies from the prophets of old, he added, "There must be an act that dramatizes the shameful."[11]

Shortly thereafter, sixteen clergy, students, a woman in a wheelchair, and several activists prayed, sang, and chanted in front of the state legislative building. When they refused to leave, police escorted them out with their hands zip-tied behind their backs. As the bus whisked the detainees away, their supporters chanted after it: "Revolutionary love!"

News coverage was scant. The crowd had been small, but committed. Still, the movement grew. Barber returned the next week with eighty demonstrators, including lawyers, doctors, and grandmothers. Thirty were arrested. Moral Mondays had begun in earnest, and every Monday thereafter, the number of protesters present at the statehouse grew by the thousands.

The coalition modeled what Rev. Barber called "moral fusion"—a term that describes the fusion coalition of Black Republicans and Populist Party members that came together in North Carolina in the nineteenth century to enhance voting rights and increase taxes to fund public education. Barber was assembling a coalition that united various issues and people of different faiths and of no faith. The movement also prioritized stories from impacted people.[12]

Having organized against extremism in North Carolina in the years prior to Trump's election, Rev. Barber was familiar with the use of voter suppression tactics used first in his home state, then replicated in additional states[13] with help from the corporate-funded American Legislative Exchange Council (ALEC).[14] Voter suppression tactics, reminiscent of the Jim Crow South, had resulted in the election of a white supremacist.

Rev. Barber spoke in sermons about how the United States was in need of a third Reconstruction.

The first Reconstruction, created to guarantee freed slaves gained their rights, followed the Civil War and was crushed when Congress allowed the prior leaders of the Confederacy to regain control and begin a reign of terror known as Jim Crow segregation.[15] The second Reconstruction—the Civil Rights movement—was partially pushed back as the following decades witnessed the steady erosion of voting rights and desegregation, as well as the rise of the criminal industrial complex—a New Jim Crow. Now we were in need of a third Reconstruction, driven by a moral fusion coalition as Rev. Barber calls for, and a resurrected Poor People's Campaign that picks up where Martin Luther King Jr. left off.

Rev. Barber reminds us that white supremacy is not new in America. It is not only alive and well, but resurgent. Barber demonstrates how an accurate spiritual assessment of our history, including our most recent history, can convict and spiritually enliven us with a vision for who we might become if we unite around our shared values. Such analysis and spiritual reflection could power a movement led by the outcry of marginalized people. By forging diverse coalitions and lifting up our moral voices, by putting our bodies on the line if need be in nonviolent, direct moral action, we could be part of God's movement in the world for justice.

HOW WE RESIST
"Remember you were once slaves and I freed you" is one of the most oft-repeated commands in Scripture. In Chapter 3, I focused on the second half of this statement: that God freed slaves. But I believe the word "Remember," in and of itself, is a

command. Indeed, for many Jews, this verse about remembering God freed them is considered a command. Remembering and reflecting on human history should be right up there with other disciplines, like prayer.

God charges us to have historical empathy. In other words, the faithful are to examine history from the reality of those who were at the bottom of the power pyramid—the slaves, the strangers, the immigrants, the poor, the widows. This is how God is revealed to us. This frees us from the deception of inevitability, this naïve idea that humanity is always progressing. Instead, Scripture teaches us to be vigilant so we can help advance God's vision for humanity.

Remembering helps us grow in several ways. For one thing, it reveals what we need to confess. My wealth as a white person was built by the labor of African Americans and on the confiscated land of Native Americans. Quite literally. I learned recently that one of my ancestors was the governor who signed the orders for the Trail of Tears so whites could take over Cherokee lands despite federal treaties guaranteeing their sovereignty. Most of the families around where I grew up got their wealth—homes, businesses, properties—from slavery or Jim Crow, which entitled them legally to cheap labor and land-grabs. Although I personally did not do these things, I still benefit, even today. I owe a debt that can never be fully repaid, but one I need to address by being willing to let go of my privilege.

Remembering also alerts us to the cycles of history: Victories won are not forever. They must be preserved. Conversely, oppression does not last forever, no matter how entrenched the system—people before us have defeated the odds and so can we. As we look at history, there is plenty to discourage us, but there are also incredible stories of diverse coalitions that defeated all odds to establish justice. When we sanitize history to avoid feeling uncomfortable, we deprive ourselves of knowing just how daunting the task ahead felt to these pioneers. John Lewis did not know when he marched across the Edmund Pettus Bridge on Bloody Sunday that he would live to be a congressman or that the act would lead to passage of the Voting Rights Act. When we dig deep into history, we learn from the bravery, the strategies, and the shortcomings of those who went before us.

Remembering can help communities expose the truth of their oppression and suffering, enabling us to take hold of our futures. While attending the World Conference Against Racism in Durban, South Africa, in 2001, I participated in a Truth and Reconciliation-related effort to support women who had experienced sexual violence at the hands of apartheid. Each woman told her story to a compassionate jury of women who recorded the details. At the end of the story, the room wailed together. After a time of lament, prayer, and laying of hands, the women led us in boisterous songs and dances of recovery. I'm sure this was only one milestone on the road to healing, yet the power of being heard, of releasing the truth, helped break the stranglehold of violence in their lives. It also helped the women shape a policy agenda working with elected officials who attended the events.

God gave us the spiritual discipline of remembrance to interrupt the dangerous slide into authoritarianism. As authoritarians incite hate and divide the people, congregations can themselves be democracy-building catalysts. Schools shy away from teaching history because history is controversial. Perhaps congregations need to step in through study groups and curricula, through hosting our own Truth and Reconciliation Commissions.

Many communities are doing so with the help of antiracism materials. Many have started book clubs to better understand where we are at this point in history. By learning in community, we can further challenge ourselves and discern how the spirit will lead us in our own Exodus moment.

Discussion Questions

1. Look again at Samuel's warning to the Israelites. Do you see aspects of that warning reflected in our own society today?
2. How have you seen the four steps to autocracy at work in the United States today or over the past few decades? Do you believe we live in a democracy?
3. What strategies might you glean from Rev. Barber's leadership?

CHAPTER 5
Hearing the Cries of the Oppressed

Human beings are so made that the ones who do the crushing feel nothing; it is the person crushed who feels what is happening. Unless one has placed oneself on the side of the oppressed, to feel with them, one cannot understand.
—Simone Weil

From early childhood, I found the Bible full of mystery, power, and splendor. I vividly remember flipping through my first children's Bible and gazing at the Disney-like palaces and temples of King Solomon. Somehow, they seemed out of place next to the pictures of Moses outraged at the golden calf, of Jesus holding fishes and loaves to feed the hungry multitudes, turning over tables, and hanging on a cross.

When I was ten, I went a little deeper, leading my school friends into an exploration of Ecclesiastes, the "book of wisdom," to see what mystical powers we might tap into.

I recall being baffled by the first verse of Ecclesiastes 1: "Meaningless! Meaningless! Utterly meaningless! Everything is meaningless (NIV)." A cynicism and numbness hung over the book. I felt disappointed. I closed the Bible. These did not seem like words of wisdom. They reminded me of the boy down the block who had everything, but was always depressed. He felt spiritually and emotionally empty, though materialistically he was full. In a voice full of cynicism and self-pity, Solomon complains repeatedly about the world, yet concludes suffering and oppression are inevitable (Eccles. 8:4): "Since a king's word is supreme who can say to him, 'What are you doing?'" Hope in God dœsn't lead to change and freedom; faith is merely a way to console oneself.

Even then, I much preferred the energized, evocative songs of the prophets who demanded repentance for the injustices of kings and the citizenry alike. In comparison, Ecclesiastes sounded off-key. The prophets such as Jeremiah and Amos speak with passion. Their cries of pain and hope pierce through the armor of denial, apathy, and corruption they rail against. The Psalms, as well, like prophetic pœtry (many of them written by King David, who was Solomon's father), are similarly full of emotion: fear, anguish, regret, repentance, joy, hope, relief, gratitude. These texts were full of pathos. But they also spoke of a hope that came from seeking God.

A closer look at the lessons of King Solomon reveals not the august leader of children's Bibles and Renaissance paintings, but the story of a ruler gone astray—a king seduced by power and wealth. A king who must be reminded by God what leadership means. It is a cautionary tale passed down through the generations to warn us that to stray from the Sinai covenant is to suffer the natural consequences that erupt from failing to love God and neighbor.

I have come to see the story of Solomon and his Temple as a cautionary tale about the unacceptable costs of authoritarianism and empire rather than the story of a wise ruler. This is the story of what happens when a nation ignores God's charge at Sinai to share power and reject inequality of any kind.

The prophets that arose during this period challenged the royal reality—the royal narrative—of King Solomon. They broke through the numbness and callousness of the wealthy and "successful" empire he created, crying out against the suffering that the king, in his greed, had created. Their lament dismantled the political spectacle of wealth, success, and power that Solomon had created and revealed a nation torn apart by deep inequality. These laments agitated the nation to resume its path to liberation.

Let's look at this story through the visit of the queen of Sheba in I Kings 10: 1-13b.[1]

Our Past: Through the Eyes of a Queen and Her Child

As the queen of Sheba, I usually have people come to me, but I made the long journey to see if the rumors about King Solomon's growing wealth were true. If they were, I would have a new trading partner and political ally.

Truth be told, I did not want to give voice to it, but something more was pulling me there. This Yahweh I'd heard about was a strange god indeed. Was it true, what they said, that this God demands justice—not just for nobility, but for everyone? Never before had I heard of a god that actually abhorred slavery. Could an empire exist without slavery?

I felt silly in my sentimentality, but ever since my son was born, I must admit, I had become soft. The love I feel for him has clouded my judgment. My father would not have approved. "Never let your feelings or even your compassion lead," he had taught me. "You cannot indulge in such luxuries if you are to stay in power." My head, not my heart, must win the day.

Despite that, I picture my son's gaze as I rock him to sleep. So trusting. I look down into his face as he drinks me in, as though my very presence is what keeps him alive.

But I struggled with the fear that this would not serve me as a leader. I could not see how I could succeed unless others feared me as they feared the gods. Indeed, they must treat me as a god!

Or could I? Was there another way to lead? Could I lead as a mother? Could I lead from compassion? Or would I be overthrown?

When I see the beggar children around my city, crying from hunger, my heart does ache for them and their empty bellies. I feel compelled to gather them up in my arms—sweat, lice, tears, and all. I see in their eyes my own son's as he looks up from my breast.

My court assumed my visit to Solomon was solely about expanding our influence through an alliance. But I had a clandestine mission: to discover who the God was who hears the cries of children and of slaves.

As we ate dinner, Solomon regaled me with stories of how Yahweh led the Israelites out of Egypt.

"God parted the rivers of the Nile so we could escape. Pharaoh's men were drowned as they tried to follow." He smirked.

Then he described their exploits in the wilderness and how Yahweh provided them with a mysterious food from the heavens and water from a desert rock.

He was drunk, not only on wine but the stories of his people. "At Mount Sinai, Yahweh made a covenant with us." His eyes were ablaze as he channeled the voice of Yahweh: "I will make you a nation of priests and a holy nation!"

He recovered from this momentary passion. His eyes dim, he took a sip of wine to compose himself.

"What does this mean?" I asked, leaning in.

His eyes lowered.

"A nation set apart," he said. "A nation with a special mission."

I responded, perhaps a little too enthusiastically, "Your God Yahweh is awesome! The eternal love Yahweh has for your people is made clear by your leadership on behalf of justice and righteousness (I Kings 10:9)?"

"Yes," he said, his eyes smiling. "Ready for your tour now?"

While touring the Temple, he took my hand. Even as a queen myself, I had seen nothing like it.

Then, as we rounded a corner to one of the newer projects still under construction, my jaw dropped again, this time in horror at the sight of hundreds of slaves working on the new residence for the king's many wives. Children were begging in the streets. A slave, off to the side, was being beaten.

Does this God that Solomon speaks of truly hear the cries of those who suffer? Or is this an almighty tyrant like all the others?

He saw my gaze fixed on this slave. He lifted my chin toward his face, and smiled with hunger in his eyes.

I found him irresistible. I hoped he could not read my thoughts. *This man is caught between the ways of the world and the God he loves. Which value will win out?*

My hopes and ambitions undaunted, I smiled and kissed him.

UNDERSTANDING THE TEXT
God had forewarned a king would use his power to oppress. Solomon is the ultimate fulfillment of this warning.

In I Kings 9: 3-9, Solomon finishes building the Temple. The moment is so important that God appears directly to Solomon—the second of only two such occasions when God comes into the presence of a human. Here is what God says:

> "I have heard the prayer and plea you have made before me; I have consecrated this temple which you have built by putting my Name there forever. My eyes and my heart will always be there.
> "As for you, if you walk before me in integrity of heart and uprightness, as David your father did, and do all I command and observe my decrees and laws, I will establish your royal throne over Israel forever . . . But if you or your sons turn away, and worship other Gods (rather than the God who freed you from Egypt) . . . I will cut off Israel from the land."

This is hardly a ringing endorsement of Solomon's great achievement. The focus of the encounter is on the Sinai covenant rather than the Temple. It is as though the spectacle of the Temple does not match up with God's charge at Sinai. Perhaps it could have been, for God says, "My eyes and my heart will always be there." But given the appalling disconnect between reality and symbol, God focuses less on celebrating and more on reminding Solomon of the blessings and curses established by the Mosaic covenant (I Kings 9:6–9). God redirects Solomon to God's priority of leading a nation governed by the ethic of loving one's neighbor. "If you fail me, Israel will become a taunt among all peoples, this house (the Temple) a heap of ruins."

The subheading "Solomon's Splendor" applied to this section of Scripture was given by more-modern editors of the Bible who had a particular viewpoint. More adequate subtitles might be: "Solomon Abandons Sinai Covenant" (1 Kings 10:14–29); followed by "Solomon Builds an Empire" (1 Kings 11:1–13); "Inequality Leads to Rebellion" (1 Kings 11:14–40).

Following the consecration of the Temple, Solomon's failures are recounted:

- the people have become "his fighting men, his government officials, his officers, his captains, and the commanders of his chariots and charioteers" (I Kings 9:22)
- the people are economically enslaved to finance Solomon's military and building projects. His so-called splendor is built on a new type of slavery (I Kings 4:6, I Kings 9:15)
- slave labor and genocide (which the people erroneously saw as God-commanded) have built the Temple for the God who hates slavery; those "whom the Israelites were unable to destroy completely—these Solomon conscripted for slave labor (I Kings 9:21)."2

These failures match up line by line with the warning Samuel delivered when the people asked for a king, which we discussed in Chapter 4 of this book:

> *He will take your sons and make them serve with his chariots and horses . . .*
> *He will take the best of your fields and vineyards and olive groves and give them to his attendants . . .*
> *He will take a tenth of your flocks . . .*
> *And you yourselves will become his slaves.*

According to this checklist, Solomon was the fulfillment of God's warning relayed through the prophet Samuel.[3]

After Solomon's death, the people went to Solomon's son Rehoboam and requested that things be rectified (1 Kings 12:4): "Your father put a heavy yoke on us, but now lighten the harsh labor and the heavy yoke he put on us, and we will serve you." Rehoboam had a chance to repent here, to return to the covenant and set Israel down the right path, but he refused. He bought the royal reality—hook, line, and sinker. Israel was plunged into civil war.

In demanding a king, the people of Sinai had given up on what God offered: a world where everyone could flourish; a world where all rule together and show other nations a new way to exist; a life following a God who loves them and who takes away their fear and material greed by giving them the guideposts of Sinai to follow. By the time of Solomon, Israel was at the pinnacle of its wealth and military might. But the Israelites were condemned to lives of misery.

In replacing Sinai's economics of equality with the economics of affluence, the politics of justice with the politics of oppression, Solomon had made the God of freedom out to be more like a god of the Egyptian reality. Weakened first through Solomon's disavowal of the Mosaic covenant, then through civil war, the northern kingdom was destroyed and Judea was carried into exile by the Babylonians. The Temple was destroyed (Psalm 137:1): By the rivers of Babylon, they sat down and wept.

A LESSON FOR US

After all of this failure, Solomon must have had a great public relations team to have gone down in history as the splendorous, wise king. Walter Brueggemann writes that empires maintain control over a disenfranchised and oppressed citizenry by convincing them that that the royal reality is unassailable.[4] Institutions, symbols, rhetoric, political spectacle, and violence shape the royal reality. It serves to convince the populace of royal legitimacy and benevolence. It helps the empire maintain utter control. Because the reality of those living under such oppressive regimes does not match up with the royal narrative or spectacle enacted before them, they find themselves in an "eternal now," where they see no future—the future, in effect, "collapses" into the present. Every day is more of the same: the drudgery of struggling to survive; of never pulling ahead, no matter what you do.

Ecclesiastes, the "book of wisdom" attributed to Solomon, captures this condition well (Eccles. 8:2–7): "Obey the king . . . Do not stand up for a bad cause . . . Whoever obeys his command will come to no harm, there is a proper time and procedure for every matter, though a man's misery weighs heavily upon him." The verse speaks eloquently to the royal reality that demands loyalty to its procedures, to its bureaucratic institutions, no matter the misery these exact. To succeed, an empire must ensure its subjects feel resistance is futile. These are the words of a law-and-order king, urging submission to one's own suffering as immutable. Contrary to God's promise at Sinai that God is the freer of slaves, Solomon implies that even God is untroubled by it all (Eccles. 8:8).

Echoing Brueggemann's thinking on the eternal now, historian Timothy Snyder writes about a "politics of eternity." Societies moving toward totalitarianism become trapped in the view that the future is just more of the present, that there are no alternatives, and therefore nothing can really be done.[5] Eternity politicians manufacture crises and manipulate fear. They deny truth and use spectacle instead. Rather than focus on policy fixes and systemic change to accommodate the needs of their people, eternity politicians create a sense of us versus them, friends against enemies, in order to distract and control their citizens. The reality and suffering remain unaddressed by practical solutions despite the wealth of those at the top. Instead, leaders enact a game of political spectacle designed to overwhelm the senses, numb and confuse the populace, and distract through demonizing the other.

Both Brueggemann and Snyder assert that "eternity rulers" deny passion—the ability to empathize with another's pain. The religion of such empires is merely an opiate designed to control and deny the suffering of the people. It serves the power and glory of an empire that can do no wrong.[6]

In the Bible, prophets step into this royal reality and disrupt it by giving voice to passion—that is, suffering— that has long been denied. They resurrect empathy through their public lament, weeping for those harmed and condemning those responsible. They expose the truth about empire and hear the pain of its people and, in doing so, they disrupt the royal spectacle and return people to their senses. Once this occurs, the people are ready and able to hear a new vision: that a new world is possible. The prophet returns them to who they are— the nation called at Sinai to be a nation of priests. A new Exodus journey is begun.

America Today: Seeing the Royal Reality of Today

It is not too hard to see a royal reality shaping our own culture. Politicians, news reports, and popular culture dangle before us a vision of American success that is disconnected from our lived reality. The disconnect between the good news reported by our leaders and real-life suffering leads to mass despair and outrage often simmering beneath the surface.

Before the pandemic and economic collapse, economic reports celebrated soaring stock prices, low unemployment rates, and increased consumer confidence. During the initial stages of the pandemic, President Trump suggested that the virus would just disappear. Once the economy began to reopen, the president celebrated a near-full economic recovery. The pain of the people was denied.

A closer look at the economy would reveal that for the past several decades, American economic inequality has risen to levels not seen since just before the Great Depression. A large percentage of Americans were either underemployed, not paid a living wage, and/or denied benefits like health care and retirement. Basic goods and services—education, pensions, health care, transport, parental leave, vacations—all have been nonexistent as our government is weakened by corporate lobbyists urging deregulation of powerful corporations and defunding via tax cuts for the wealthiest .1 percent.

America ostensibly celebrates the Civil Rights Movement's legacy through Black History Month and MLK Day. Yet we fail to address the facts that Emory University professor and *New York Times* bestselling author Carol Miller has documented:

> *The hard-fought victories of the Civil Rights Movement caused a reaction that stripped Brown of its power, severed the jugular of the Voting Rights Act, closed off access to higher education, poured crack cocaine into the inner cities, and locked up more black men proportionally than even apartheid-era South Africa.*[7]

The everyday stress of living is further burdened by endless social media, news alerts, texting, and email, all of which keep us hooked up to sensationalized news cycles and spectacles made even emptier by widespread disinformation—lies, that is. There is no time to be, to think, to care, to know who and whose we are. It is hard to feel when we are bombarded and overstimulated.

The Trump presidency has brought this to all new heights, thriving on distraction, disinformation, vitriolic tweeting, and bombarding us with headlines that feel like they belong in a dystopian film. The press, accustomed to reporting on everything a president does and eager for ratings, pumps attention even higher. Attempts to rein in the president only escalate rather than alleviate conflict. If he is accused of colluding with Russians, he accuses his opponents of the same. When he is admonished by Twitter for posting disinformation, he threatens to censor and restrict free speech, muddying the waters for those trying to make sense of it all in their busy lives.

Prosperity gospel leaders surround the president, promoting his claim that he is God's anointed. The religion that funnels wealth into the hands of its leaders peddles the lie that sufferers will find relief if they donate more of their meager incomes to get right with God. To suffer is to have done something to deserve suffering. Trump's royal court, staffed by false prophets like the prosperity gospel preacher Paula White and Christian nationalist pastor Robert Jeffress, absolves the president and his followers of the responsibility to hear the cries of those in need and get to the source of injustice.[8] This serves the empire very well.

What can stop this royal reality, which began before President Trump, which has been taken to new heights, and which will certainly continue into the future at one level or another, no matter the outcome of the 2020 election?

A LESSON FOR US
In the Bible, it is prophetic imagination that breaks through the royal reality. The prophets bring public expression to the fears and terrors that have been denied so long and suppressed so deeply we don't know they are there.[9] The prophets speak

forthrightly of the "deathliness" that hovers over us with candor and anguish rather than with rage or cheap grace.[10]   Today prophets are taking to the streets, forcing America to own up to the utter failure of our nation's criminal justice system that includes a police force allowed to murder with impunity Black women and men. Their lament is shaking loose decades of denial by systems blinded by whiteness. Their vision of defunding police, and putting much-needed resources instead back into communities, is pushing cities to shift their entire paradigm around what it takes to build safe and healthy communities. It is up to us to hear and join their cries for change.

Modern Models: Seeing Them, Hearing Their Cries
George Floyd begged for mercy while a police officer knelt on his neck for over eight minutes: "Please, I can't breathe!" He cried for his mother as he was passing from this world to the next, the life ebbing from his body. The officer stared placidly, hand in his pocket, at nearby witnesses who begged, "Check his pulse! Please check his pulse!" Officer Derek Chauvin ignored their cries. He refused to move as Floyd gradually stopped crying out because he no longer breathed.

Days later, a young Black man stood in Lafayette Square, the park in front of the White House. He was face-to-face with a police officer in riot gear. Standing shoulder to shoulder with other young people, protesting the brutal murder of George Floyd at the hands of a Minneapolis police officer, the man belted out his lament: "You don't feel my pain, bro?" His moral outrage boiled over. "All I'm asking for is reform, bro. Is that too much to ask for?"[11] The officer remained impassive, staring straight through him. The protester leaned forward slightly, his eyes laserlike on the shielded face in front of him, trying to penetrate the riot gear and the officer's callousness. The young man's voice cracked. "Please . . . tell me!" He was determined to make this officer hear him, see him, care about him. He knelt, put his hand over his mouth, and sobbed fiercely, inconsolable.

Minutes later, without warning, tear gas, flash bombs, and rubber bullets were fired at the nonviolent crowd. Panicked protesters and journalists were slammed by police shields. People fled in all directions. Protesters of all ages and races groped through a crowd, barely able to see, their eyes burning from the gas irritants. Some clutched their stomachs and limbs, bleeding and bruised by rubber bullets.

A priest and several seminarians who had been working with activists to provide hospitality and medical care ended up caught in the brutal crackdown. The priest tended to the wounded, then fled as the police pressed toward the medic station. The priest later tweeted, "He would have had to step over our medical supplies we left behind because we were being teargassed!"[12]

Once the front patio of the church was cleared, the US president sauntered in and postured with a Bible held up in his right hand like a trophy. There was no compassion in his face. It was a face that communicated, "I am immovable. I do not and will not see your pain. Obey me or I will crush you with my power." The administration's propagandists circulated only his image of a leader posing for a photo op, and nothing of the brutality that occurred just moments before. He had invalidated their pain. Without praying, without speaking to the pain of the people, the pretender king retreated placidly to his fortress. A reporter observed, "He just walked by himself up into the gate . . . all alone. . . . Somehow everyone fell back. . . . He stood alone, almost godlike, and just walked to the White House."[13]

The Episcopal bishop who presides over this church, Mariann Budde, later said, "I was outraged. My major outrage was the abuse of sacred symbols and sacred texts. There was no acknowledgment of grief, no acknowledgment of wounds. There was no attempt to heal. The Bible calls us to our highest aspirations and he used it as a prop." The royal reality was on full display in the denial of grief and terror, in the use of sacred symbols to assert imperial control.

In the days following, clergy and lay leaders continued to pour into the streets to reclaim sacred space and symbols, to bind up wounds, to hear the cries and deepen their plans of action.

The protests sparked by George Floyd's murder were a tipping point. For decades, the problems of police brutality and white supremacist violence have gone unaddressed despite mass protests, despite studies validating policies designed to end it. George Floyd, Breonna Taylor (a medical worker killed by police in her own home), and Ahmaud Arbery (murdered while jogging) are just the tip of the iceberg. Many African Americans live in fear that they or their children will suffer the same fate at the hands of those who are supposed to protect all of us.

The same police officer who smiled and gave me a kind warning after pulling me over for making an illegal turn at a red light may terrorize a Black person who does the same. As a white woman, I do not live in fear that my son will be shot by police or vigilantes for wearing a hoodie or for jogging through a neighborhood. Trapped in the privilege that our skin color grants us, white people do not know about or accept Black realities caused by racism. White people are spiritually blind and atrophied if we fail to hear George Floyd crying, "I can't breathe," and then follow those cries upstream to find what caused them. Confronting white supremacy and our role in sustaining such systems is the primary spiritual calling for white people in America today who seek to be faithful.

HOW WE RESIST

Despite being a budding activist in the nineties, I failed to fully understand the protests that broke out in 1992 after the Rodney King beating. People of color tried to explain it to me. But I had been raised to trust police. I had never encountered police, much less been degraded by them. I tried to hear, but my white brain, colored by my experience, still wondered if Rodney King had done something to "get himself in that situation." I failed to accept the pain and anger of my Black and Asian friends. I have since learned, by listening to the pain, and I am learning still.

The only way forward for all of us is to listen to the screams and accept Black realities. Rev. William Barber II, interviewed on MSNBC the weekend after the protests following George Floyd's death began, asked us all, "What is this mourning saying to America?" Like the prophets of old, he told us, "The hope is in these screams." He redirected our attention to the real source of grief: "You talk about violence. Before COVID, seven hundred people were dying a day in America because of poverty and low wealth. Eighty million were uninsured in the richest nation in the world. And then people are dying from not having PPE and being forced to work. And then you see a public lynching.

"We need to listen to these screams. We need to listen to what this mourning is saying to America. The hope is in the screams." [14]

Only in hearing the screams can we build a new America—the one we have always talked about, but never lived out.

The prophet Amos railed against those who trampled the poor and deprived them of justice in court. God told him that because of such injustice (Amos 5:16–17):

> *"There will be wailing in all the streets*
> *and cries of anguish in every public square.*
> *The farmers will be summoned to weep*
> *and the mourners to wail.*
> *There will be wailing in all the vineyards,*
> *for I will pass through your midst."*

"I will pass through your midst." *God is in the streets, in the public square, in the vineyards weeping.*

God is in the streets as I write this chapter. Those yelling, "Black Lives Matter. I can't breathe. No justice, no peace," they are prophets to us today. When we hear their cries and act so that policy makers make the necessary reforms, then, and only then, will peace follow.

The story of Solomon warns us that making God over in the image of the surrounding culture is a form of idolatry. As we look at Solomon and consider his words in Ecclesiastes, we find ourselves challenged to consider ways in which our own faith might be acculturated to a materialistic and imperialistic American culture. We find ourselves scrutinizing the ways in which we are numb and blind to the oppression around us. We see that following the cries of those who are marginalized is the way to draw near to God. Such a path requires courage. But the fruit of the journey is joy and peace as we grow close to the God of Sinai.

Discussion Questions

1. How did the story of Solomon strike you when you first heard it?
2. Read Ecclesiastes 8 and Amos 5. What differences do you see? Try reading them out loud. Dramatize them. What do you feel?
3. What laments have you been blind to in your life? Where has your heart been opened?

CHAPTER 6
Following Women of Color

I am not free while any woman is unfree, even when her shackles are very different from my own.

—— Audre Lorde

"Women can't have as much rights as men, 'cause Christ wasn't a woman!" Where did your Christ come from?

—Sojourner Truth

"Women should not teach men."
"You sound shrill."
"You should smile more often."
"No one will believe you."
"You might get raped. Be careful."
"I would vote for her, but I think she is unelectable."
"You don't really belong here."
"Forgive him, that is just how men are."

These are messages I've heard and internalized for as long as I can remember. Such thoughts are planted in most, if not all, of us by the sins of sexism (a belief that women are inferior) and misogyny (the system that enforces that belief).

These views have been justified by Scripture throughout history. Verses like, "Women be silent" (I Cor. 14:34) are thrown at us when we try to lead. The ancient baptismal creed "In Christ there is no . . . slave nor free, male nor female, for we are all one in Christ Jesus" (Gal. 3:28) is ignored.

In an era dominated by patriarchal laws and norms, both the Hebrew and Christian Scriptures begin with women who call to account their respective tyrants—the pharaohs and Caesars—of their day. These stories of women's leadership have often been erased by men who seek to control memory and meaning. Even so, the truth that emerges from the Bible is that women often are the first ones who respond to God's call. Women are at the front lines of God's movement in the world. Women hear God, and women lead.

God's intervention in history begins with women. And yet, for most of history, the Church has limited women's leadership roles and minimized women's experiences of injustice, often ignoring cases of sexual abuse. The church has failed to champion the biblical vision for equality.

It is time for us to reclaim our rightful role and reclaim our radical faith traditions.

Our Past: Women on the Front Lines for Jesus

You surely have certain perceptions that come to mind when you hear my name: Mary Magdalene. But let me tell you about my experience. You may know I led the march to Jesus' tomb, forcing my way through the crowd as quickly as I could. Joanna, Mary (the mother of James), and some others followed me. But do you know what was at stake for us? Our courage was fueled by rage over what the state had done to Jesus. I knew we were taking a risk, but we had no time to second-guess ourselves.

We ignored the warning of the eleven remaining male

disciples. They could not remain in hiding while Jesus' body needed to be appropriately buried. Roman soldiers were looking to crack down on the movement—we knew that. But we stepped out in courage anyway.

When we reached the tomb, I froze. The other women came up behind me and saw the stone had been rolled away. Stepping cautiously forward, I whispered, "He's not here." Then louder, with a yell coming out of the depths of my soul, a mama-bear howl:

"HE'S
NOT
HERE!"

I had thought something like this could happen. The Romans had tortured Jesus and broken his body. Now they had desecrated his tomb. This was what they did to quash revolutions. They killed and desecrated the bodies of those who challenged Caesar so their followers could not rally. Jesus' revolution was more spiritual, but its implications were political. *Even more of a threat to the status quo than the Zealots,* I thought, breathing heavily and looking around, desperate to do something.

Suddenly two men appeared outside the tomb. They seemed to glow from within, such that it was hard to make them out.

Terrified, Joanna, Mary, and the others fell to the ground, but I shouted, "Where have you taken him?" The anger rose up from my core.

One of the men looked at me, puzzled and calm. "Why do you look for the living among the dead?" he asked. His expression read, "You know this, don't you?"

It dawned on me. *This* is what he was saying. Of course. We rushed back to the men's hideout. Something had shifted in me. Not only might I see Jesus again, the death and suffering wrought by the Empire was not the last word. His vision of radical inclusion—embracing the unclean woman healed by touching his cloak, the Syrophœnician woman (who challenged Jesus to hear her), the woman at the well—would be brought to the entire world.

Joanna, Mary, and I were all shaking and breathless with relief, joy, and excitement. We were covered in sweat and dust. When we arrived, our words tumbled out over each other as we rushed to tell the good news. "He's not there. He has risen! Just as he said he would!"

The disciples stared at us with scorn.

"Nonsense, get in here before you expose us all," Peter hissed, looking this way and that for signs of Roman soldiers.

We looked at each other. We saw the defiance in each other's faces. Then we turned and walked away. We would not be silenced anymore.

UNDERSTANDING THE TEXT

My friend, writer Carol Howard Merritt, recently tweeted a block-print etching of Sojourner Truth, her hand up in classic teacher pose: "For those who don't 'believe in' women preachers . . . that's like saying you don't believe in atoms. They have always existed, whether you believe in them or not."

The Jesus movement begins with women launching God's liberative plan into the world. The women defied Rome and the male disciples to proclaim that Jesus had risen. God's plan to throw the mighty from their thrones and exalt the oppressed was not thwarted.

The Gospel of Luke, like Exodus, shows God entering human history through the actions of women. Mary, the mother of Jesus, is often portrayed as meek and mild. But Luke portrays her as a partner with God.[1] Mary, unlike Sarah or Hannah in the Hebrew Scriptures, and unlike her cousin Elizabeth, was not saved from barrenness. And God did not even approach Joseph to tell him what was about to unfold. God went straight to Mary, who chose to be part of God's plan to take on tyrants. Her song has survived millennia and tells us she was much more than an incubator for the Messiah:

> God has put down the mighty from their
> thrones and exalted those of low degree;
> God has filled the hungry with good things
> And the rich God has sent empty away.
>   (Luke 1:52–53)

Her song is a song of rebellion in her Roman-occupied town.

Luke begins with Mary's song and cousin Elizabeth's visit. Elizabeth, of course, was pregnant with John the Baptist. In telling this story, Luke, the Gospel writer, is clearly echoing Chapter 1 of Exodus, in which three sets of women led a rebellion against Pharaoh. Shiphrah and Puah, the Hebrew midwives, risked their lives and refused Pharaoh's orders to kill male children. Moses' mother and his sister, Miriam, identified a new resistance strategy— they made a raft and floated the baby down the river. In a show of cross-class solidarity, Bityah, the daughter of the tyrant himself, heard Moses' cries, rescued and raised him, committing treason and risking her own privileged status. I like to think that these three sets of women were part of a fusion coalition of women that organized across tribe, class, and religion to save a people and defy an evil leader.

The fact that women led the charge against tyranny and revealed the true nature of God tells us something of God's new world order. Those who are marginalized are the ones who lead. Women are not only the ones who literally bring new life into the world, they also bring radical spiritual awakenings. God is introduced in Chapter 2 of

Exodus as the God who—like the midwives and Moses' rescuers—heard the cries of oppressed people. Scripture tells us to be like these women, for to hear the cries and act is to see the face of God.

Likewise, the women at the tomb were the first to see and believe that Jesus had overcome death. They were the first to counter the hopelessness of oppression with the belief that the radical ethic of God's love has the power to bring about resurrection. Maybe, as my friend and Sikh activist Valarie Kaur says, "the darkness of the tomb is the darkness of the womb."

The centrality of women in God's call to liberation is an essential lens for understanding Scripture. Women lead throughout the narrative: Shiphrah, Puah, Miriam, Hagar, Sarah, Ruth, Naomi, Rahab, Hannah, Deborah, Phœbe (a benefactor of early church), Priscilla (a preacher who worked with Paul), and Junia (an apostle called by Paul). Texts that seem to mandate lesser roles for women are often poorly understood—either mistranslated or taken out of context.

To give one example, most of us have been taught that Eve was made from the rib of Adam. She is, therefore, a lesser human, a derivative of Adam, made to be his "helpmate" and servant. She is made to "complement" him (since she has his rib, after all). But to read the text in the original Hebrew is to know that God makes *Adamah*—best translated "human." Then God makes Adam (note that "Adam" is a shortened version of *Adamah*) and Eve from that being. Two beings made equally from the same original material. In fact, the Hebrew word mistranslated as "helpmate" is actually used always to describe someone of equal or higher status, not lesser status.

Like Mary, Elizabeth, the women at Jesus' tomb, and the Exodus "Dream Team," we need to unite across ethnicity, religion, and privilege. To do that is about far more than overcoming differences. Those of us with power and privilege need to scrutinize our own role in systemic oppression. Otherwise, in seeking to do good, we will only do more harm.

It's time for women of faith to lead this nation forward. Yet to do so, we white women will need to take responsibility for the ways our everyday lives, leadership styles, and hoarding of power perpetuate racism. We need to reflect on our impact, listen to women of color, and follow their lead.

America Today: Race and Change

"Seeing oneself in the biblical text," as I have encouraged readers to do in this book, including in this chapter, is a two-edged sword. It is crucial to bring the biblical text into our struggles for justice and peace, while also recognizing the many differences among those in the struggle. One absolutely crucial difference is race.

For those who are deemed "white" in this country, it is often astonishing when they realize there are no "white people" in the Bible. The pictures of a blue-eyed, blond Jesus found in many white churches notwithstanding, none of the biblical actors I have mentioned in this book were of European ethnicity with a specific light-skin color.

The stories in the Bible were appropriated by the ruling classes in Europe, and they imposed their own lighter-skin color as well as their economic privilege onto the text. This propaganda was imported to American shores, and it is the genesis of the virulent white supremacist perspective that still exists today.

Those who identify as women have been oppressed in many ways. That has often led white straight women of gender privilege, i.e. cisgender women, to assume that their oppression based on gender is identical or at least similar to the oppression experienced by people of color, especially of women of color.

That is not the case. White cisgender women have power and privileges conferred by white supremacy and sexuality. This truth is too often ignored.

Historically, multiracial coalitions have set out to dismantle white supremacy and patriarchy, and yet have failed to see it through. When it came to abolitionism, women's suffrage, and civil rights, white women often failed to see the full humanity of Black women. Such efforts brought about important policy changes and strides toward freedom, but left deep wounds and fissures that prevent us from ultimately healing the core sin of racism.

White, cisgender women, like myself, are like Sarai in the Bible, who is so threatened by the growing power of her servant Hagar that she casts her out into the wilderness with her infant son, possibly to die. In a rebuke of Sarai, God makes a way out of no way for Hagar.

The week that George Floyd was killed by a police officer in Minneapolis, I saw the video of a woman in New York's Central Park threatening to call 911 on a bird-watching Black man and "tell them there's an African-American man threatening my life." The woman, Amy Cooper, was enraged because the man, Christian Cooper, asked her to put her dog on a leash in accordance with park policy. She followed through on the threat, feigning distress to the 911 dispatcher. I was horrified by how easily she escalated such a mundane conflict into a racist death threat.

The incident went viral because it was so perfectly emblematic of racism in the year 2020. This white woman (though she wore leggings and a sweater rather than a white hood and robe), when challenged by an African-American man, wielded her privilege in an act of intimidation no less explicit than a burning cross.

White women's racism often takes quieter, less dramatic, but nonetheless dangerous, forms. A plurality of white women cast their vote for Trump in 2016, and two-thirds of white evangelical women voted for him, despite his extensive record of overt bigotry. And I often wonder how many stayed home on Election Day despite the presence of an overt bigot on the ballot. Meanwhile, 98 percent of Black women and two-thirds of Latina women voted against him.

These discrepancies should cut us to the quick and cause us to examine our hearts and souls. Why do white women, time and time again, disconnect from women of color?

A LESSON FOR US

All women face hurdles that men do not face. And yet, white women, like myself, benefit from the oppression of women of color. We get better health care, higher salaries, greater job security, and deference from police. I don't fear that my teenage son will be targeted or killed by police or immigration enforcement agents. I am spared women of color's everyday experiences of dismissal, distrust, and discrimination.

I'm so grateful to the Black, Latina, indigenous, and Asian women in my life who help me see this. I'm still learning, and always will be, and part of that learning is accepting that it's not women of color's job to educate me. I have to take responsibility for my own learning and my own change.

As a white woman, I know I have much to repent for. It is time for us to listen and do our own work of self-examination about our privilege and power.

We cannot merely think that because we aren't overt bigots, we are antiracist. Racism isn't a feeling. Racism is a system that feeds economic power and privilege to a storied few who happen to have a white skin color.

We can only eliminate racism by letting go of the power and benefits of whiteness. We need to yield leadership to women of color rather than take more for ourselves. We will need to be convicted by the fact that our neighborhoods, organizations, schools, and congregations economically benefit from modern segregation. While our children go to "good schools" and can walk safely through a park wearing a hoodie, children of color have no such privilege. And unless we are working to dismantle this systemic racism, we are part of the problem.

Our shared Christian faith teaches us to hear the cries of injustice, examine our own sin, and act. Today white Christian women must pledge to hear the challenge to our whiteness posed by women of color, knowing that this is how God will lead us forward into a new vision of how to live together.

Modern Models: A World Where Women and Families Can Flourish

Recently I helped lead a two-day dialogue with a diverse group of pro-life and pro-choice women tired of politicians making abortion into a partisan wedge issue while failing to address the abysmal state of women's reproductive care in the United States. I found there was a lot more that unites us than divides us.

For one thing, we all agree that it is unacceptable that maternal mortality in the US is the highest in the industrialized world, that Black women in the US die during childbirth at three to four times the rate of white mothers, and that it is safer to give birth in Bosnia or Kuwait than in California.[2]

In an act of sheer hypocrisy, the Republican-initiated Affordable Care Act (ACA) replacements proposed in 2017 would have increased the costs of women's pregnancy care, as well as the cost of contraception. It would have allowed states to define ACA-mandated essential health benefits in Medicaid plans—in many cases eliminating coverage for pregnancy, labor, and neonatal care. This is a party that calls itself pro-life?

There has to be a better way forward that fully supports women and their children. Again, it is women of color who are leading the way.

In 1994, a group of Black women gathered in Chicago to discuss reproductive health challenges faced by their communities. The women's rights movement—led by middle-class and wealthy white women—was blind to the needs of women of color and other marginalized women. The Chicago meeting gave birth to the movement for reproductive justice. This growing movement fights for the right to have children and parent those children in safe and sustainable communities, as well as the right to not have children and to have bodily autonomy.

What a paradigm shift this approach was for me when I first heard it. It lifts up a vision for the kind of world we need to create—a world where women can safely have children and see them flourish.

One of the movement leaders, Sister Song, shares on their website that the movement focuses on access rather than choice: access to contraception, comprehensive sex education, STI prevention and care, alternative birth options, adequate prenatal and pregnancy care, domestic violence assistance, adequate wages to support their families, safe homes, and so much more. So many of these are services white women take for granted.

Whatever our own feelings about abortion, when we look at the issue through an economic and racial justice lens, we end up having to address inconsistencies. Are elected officials pro-life if they allow nursing babies to be separated from their mothers at the border? What if they refuse to support the Violence Against Women Act or to end pregnancy discrimination?

We all know what families need to thrive: wages that enable them to support children; paid sick leave so that they don't lose a job when a child gets sick (nearly half of American workers do not have paid sick leave), and affordable, quality child care so they can work as needed.

Christian women from pro-life and pro-choice camps are increasingly finding common cause. Christian writer and activist Lisa Sharon Harper led pro-life women in "A Call to Pause the Culture Wars."[3] In this era, when some white evangelicals have turned a blind eye to racism while focusing on abortion, Harper and others have pointed out that the Christian Right was born out of opposition to integration, not pro-life concerns.[4]

In the wake of a 2019 Alabama legislation banning abortion with no exceptions for rape and incest, many Christian women spoke out for the first time about the need to trust women to make moral decisions that affect their bodies and their families' well-being. To give one example, in a *USA Today* piece titled "I was 12 years old and pregnant. Alabama's abortion ban bill would punish girls like me," Christian author Shannon Dingle concluded: "This is why abortion can't be dictated by legislators. This is why abortion decisions must be made individually, between a woman and her doctor."[5]

Pro-life and pro-choice aren't mutually exclusive categories. Some of the women at the dialogue I led identified as both. Amid our moral wrestling, we built consensus around the importance of trusting women's moral agency to make sound decisions in consultation with doctors and their spiritual leaders. I hope we can focus on holding politicians accountable for ensuring women and families get the support they need so every pregnancy can be an occasion to celebrate and every woman has what she needs to thrive and raise a healthy family.

HOW WE RESIST

Women throughout Scripture and history have led the way. Since 2016, we have seen a record number of women elected to congress and to state houses, many of them women of color. In 2017, Danica Rœm became the first openly transgender person elected and seated in a state legislature.[6] Women voters have been heralded for their record turnout in elections, and women organizers have led the charge. Women now lead many of the religious organizations working for just policies. My organization has a senior leadership team of all women and 40 percent women of color. Dr. Leslie Copeland-Tune is the COO of the National Council of Churches. Stosh Cotler leads Bend the Arc: a Jewish Partnership for Justice. Rabbi Jill Jacobs leads T'ruah: the Rabbinic Call for Human Rights. Rev. Traci Blackmon leads the public policy work of the United Church of Christ. The list could go on.

The work of women of faith is more critical than ever, but significant structural change will not happen unless the structure of power and privilege within our movement—funding streams, leadership choices, and more—happens as well. This cannot be tokenism. We have to "be the change we wish to see in the world," as Mahatma Gandhi said, not merely as individuals but as a movement.

Neither of the two major political parties in this country embodies this structural change, and both must be challenged at the core. White privilege and white supremacy have played an enormous role in dividing women. That has to be rejected, not with lip service, but with a restructuring of the power within diverse coalitions for change.

We who identify as women can make an enormous difference in challenging this society to make substantive and lasting change for peace and justice.

I do not have all the answers, but I do know the time is now.

Discussion Questions

1. What are your favorite Scriptures about women's leadership? Which ones disturb you?
2. Where have you seen women lead the way in history and in your community? Do women have unique gifts?
3. Does race divide women? If so how, and how do we overcome this?

CHAPTER 7
Knowing Your Text

Post-truth is pre-fascism.
—Dr. Timothy Snyder

Before mass leaders seize the power to fit reality to their lies, their propaganda is marked by its extreme contempt for facts as such, for in their opinion fact depends entirely on the power of man who can fabricate it.
—Hannah Arendt

George Orwell's *1984* depicted a world in which a government controlled the populace through two-way screens and propaganda campaigns. In America today, the government does not control the media; corporations with political and economic interests do. Many state and local papers have failed in the past twenty years. And the Internet, once thought to be primarily a democratizing force, presents new challenges. Forty percent of the US population gets news through Facebook. And yet, unlike any actual news outlet, Facebook has little commitment to ensuring the accuracy of content. According to the FBI, Facebook was the platform for a massive propaganda campaign in the 2016 presidential elections.[1] And studies have shown YouTube's algorithm pushes viewers toward content that is more extreme than what they started with—or to incendiary content in general.[2] In some instances, groups were able to incite riots using altered YouTube video.[3]

Strong democracies require people on all sides to value objective information, agree on at least some self-evident truths, and share the moral value of honesty. Without shared facts and commitment to truth, it is impossible to decide on policies that support the general welfare and balance competing interests. Authoritarian and totalitarian regimes bend people to the regime's will by defining what is and is not truth. Today democratic backsliding may come about through the manipulation of media, not by government but by extremist groups, corporate interests, and foreign actors. These may be operating separately or in tandem with those in political power.

Scripture has a lot to say about truth. Unfortunately, we often see "truth" as referencing the truth about Jesus. Instead, I invite us to explore truth as the liberative truth of the Gospel revealed in Jesus. This truth enables us to fight back against imperial propaganda.

Our Past: No Justice for the Innocent

The man healed my mother, and now he is standing trial. For what? I wondered.

Rebellion was in the air, and everyone was suspect. We were living under a curfew. Pilate, the governor, had brutally squashed any opposition to the ways of the Romans. No one was allowed to gather. Despite the pleadings of my mother, I set out for the trial, hoping that Pilate would rule in favor of this healer, Jesus. If nothing else, I would show my support. It was the least I could do.

Perhaps it was futile, as mother said, but Jesus showed me that every act of love has ripple effects, even if we can't always see them. Living under occupation had made me forget that. We were all so fearful. We kept our heads down and forgot each other's faces. If our eyes were on the muck, we could not lift our gazes to the heavens.

I wanted to have hope. Jesus had not called for violence or armed insurrection. He taught me to turn the other cheek, to help the least of these. Was this so wrong? Maybe Pilate would dismiss the charges.

Jesus was answering questions. He looked sad but calm. "My kingdom is not of this realm."

I heard Pilate say, "Aha, then you *are* a king!" He was trying to corner Jesus. I held my breath.

"*You* say that I am. I have come into the world to testify to the truth."

I had a sinking feeling.

"What is truth?" Pilate smiled cynically.

Now my blood ran cold. The Roman Empire was gradually taking over all aspects of our daily lives. Many were worshiping Caesar as Lord—it was hard not to. Pilate was demanding absolute loyalty to the Roman Empire. You couldn't even buy bread to eat without bowing to this megalomaniac.

To resist imperial reality, we called Jesus—not Caesar—Lord and King. We had sung Hosannas and waved palm branches as he rode into Jerusalem on a donkey. It had felt good to morally rebuke the Romans and their puppets who left our people destitute.

But Jesus was no Zealot. He was not armed. He had merely taught us to see each other's humanity, to see that we all were neighbors. Because of Jesus, we had begun to lift our heads and reach out to each other. Neighbors were helping each other, like we once did before the occupation. My village was rebuilding its communal water system destroyed in the conquest. But even that seemed to make soldiers livid. They had destroyed it as soon as it was completed. Surely, Pilate would not find this offensive.

Next Pilate smiled, but there was no warmth in his eyes. He grunted cynically.

Pilate put the verdict to the crowd. As I looked around, I saw agents of Rome stirring up the crowd. From the back, one of them shouted, "Give us Barabbas." This was not the will of our neighbors.

Pilate nodded, and suddenly Jesus was taken away. What? It made no sense. They were releasing Barabbas. How could this nonviolent healer be more threatening to them than the robber Barabbas?

Deep down, I knew. The Roman Empire needed us to keep our eyes on the ground. To give up all hope of justice. To believe its "truth" that Caesar would reign for all eternity. Love in action was more of a threat to this empire than armed insurrection. Our limited weapons would never be a match for Roman military might, but enabling people to trust each other again, despite the poverty and brutality around them . . . now, that was a threat. Rejecting the idea that Caesar is Lord punched a hole in Rome's desire to appear invincible. Uniting the poor, forging solidarity between the Samaritans and Judeans, the wealthy few not co-opted by the Romans and the tax collectors, that was a threat to those who claimed the right to rule.

If we connected with each other, trusted each other, resisted brutality, organized our communities, everything would change in time. In my heart, I knew they could not allow this.

UNDERSTANDING THE TEXT

The historian Josephus claimed Pilate alone was responsible for Jesus' crucifixion on charges of sedition for claiming to be "King of the Jews." Yet the Gospels suggest that Pilate was reluctant and merely complying with the demands of Joseph Caiaphas, the high priest of Jerusalem. Which narrative is true?

To understand what might have been happening here, it's helpful to know how the Romans governed conquered territories. The *Pax Romana*, or Roman Peace, has often been romanticized as a time of unprecedented peace and economic progress. But a closer look reveals that Rome maintained order through a brutal criminal justice and economy that impoverished the masses and drove many into debt, bondage, and slavery for the sake of imperial expansion.

From the time of Caesar Augustus (the ruler when Jesus was born), Rome governed through what is known as the imperial cult—a totalitarian belief system that required subjects to worship Caesar as a god. The worship of the emperor extended to all areas of life in the Roman Empire. Subjects had to pay tribute to Rome. High levels of taxation and concomitant graft and corruption were required to extend and maintain Rome's splendorous and tightly controlled dominance. This economic system left the masses barely able to survive. The imposition of emperor worship required not just the worship of another as a god, but with that, a violation of the Mosaic covenant. As explored in the chapter on the golden calf, idolatry was not just the worship of other gods or Caesar, it was the worship of that which is the antithesis of Yahweh. The Roman economic system and imperial cult came into direct conflict with the community-oriented ethics of the Torah, making it impossible to implement the Sabbath and jubilee, and forcing Jews to worship the emperor and his ways. In Jesus' time, imperial cults were increasing dominance over Jewish life.

When Rome conquered Palestine, they ruled through the Jewish elites—the Herodian dynasty—and executed any who did not comply with the new regime. Roman governors appointed the Jewish high priests, such as Caiaphas, who would have served as a liaison between Roman authorities and the Jewish population. Roman prefects could demand the priests arrest and turn over Jews seen as agitators. For ten years, Caiaphas served with Pontius Pilate, so presumably they had a good relationship or Pilate would have removed him. They most likely had a method for dealing with subversives. The tensions we see between Jesus and Jewish leaders reflect the tensions between a conquered people and a ruling elite that did the bidding of Rome.

Pilate had a reputation for cruelty and the ruthless suppression of those who gave him trouble. In Jesus' time, he had sparked a protest among the Jews for smuggling in effigies of Caesar overnight. He had ruthlessly put down a rebellion against his use of Temple taxes to build a Roman aqueduct, an incident that might be related to the reference of bloodshed in Luke 13:1. It is likely that during Jesus' trial, civil unrest had again broken out in Jerusalem. The ancient historian Philo wrote around 42 C.E. in *Embassy to Gaius 302* that Pilate's tenure was associated with "briberies, insults, outrages, wanton injustices, constantly repeated executions without trial and ceaseless and grievous cruelty."[4] In other words, Pilate was not one to have reservations about executing a Jewish rabble-rouser like Jesus. Many historians attribute the softening of Pilate's image to efforts by early Christians to make their message more palatable to Roman audiences. It seems more likely that a man accustomed to brutally cracking down on unrest would have had no qualms about executing Jesus and manipulating the crowds to avoid yet another Passover rebellion. The form of execution—crucifixion—also suggests that Jesus was condemned for violating Roman, not Jewish, law.

In the Gospel of John, Pilate does not ask, "What is the truth here?" but "What is truth?" Do not mistake him for a Greek philosopher. As shown in this Gospel, we could very well conclude Pilate is saying there is no truth—truth is what an empire says it is. It would be more consistent with the Pilate of history to see that he was not interested in Jesus' guilt or innocence, but in his own personal power. In order to survive, every totalitarian regime must define what is and is not truth.

This is why the Gospel of John speaks so frequently of truth. Jesus said (John 8:32) that if you follow his teachings, "the truth will set you free." In John 8:44, those unable to accept Jesus' teachings follow Satan, who is "the father of lies." The Gospel writers suggested that Rome was under the power of the devil.[1] Jesus stands up against the devil-controlled empire and its lies, revealing God's empire *(basileia)*. It is not surprising that Pilate questions the very existence of truth, for he serves the father of lies.

Jesus, whose teachings challenged the worst aspects of Roman occupation with love and grace, who called himself "King of the Jews" in direct challenge to Caesar, and who had amassed a significant following, was a direct threat to Pilate, the law-and-order governor. Pilate asserted the imperial narrative with a brutal reminder that no one dare call himself the Son of God in direct contradiction to Caesar, who alone was god's son. And with that, no one dare challenge the exploitative economic model of Rome that channeled money to elites and criminalized the masses through debt bondage. He then set out to humiliate Jesus and assert Roman dominance by dressing him in a purple robe and crown of thorns. He then had a sign nailed to the cross that mockingly read: KING OF THE JEWS.

America Today: How Truth Dies

Observers of totalitarianism such as Victor Klemperer observed that truth dies in four modes, all of which we are witnessing today.

The first stage is open hostility to verifiable reality. In this phase, a leader simply presents lies as though they are facts.

Fact checkers report that by the third year of his term in office (just 1,055 days), President Trump made 15,413 false or misleading claims.[2] Conservative news outlets, such as Fox, report these lies, seldom questioning their veracity through investigative journalism. No longer do Americans drink from the same wells of news like they did in the days before cable. Complicating matters further, the news is driven by what makes money rather than by civic-minded journalism.

The second stage of totalitarian destruction of truth is the use of endless repetition designed to make the "fictional plausible and the criminal desirable."[3]

President Trump has, of course, perfected this mode of communication with chants like "Build the Wall" and "Lock her up," as well as the nicknames he bestows on his opponents like "sleepy Joe." Calling the Mueller investigation a "witch hunt," and repeating the patently false claim that the investigation exonerated him, enabled Trump to confuse many Americans who couldn't take time to read the actual report.

Trump's methods are a culmination of a political tactic started in the 1990s by former Speaker of the House Newt Gingrich. Gingrich urged his party to focus on message development, wedge issues (regardless of relevance or importance), and antigovernment sentiment rather than developing policy solutions based on evidence and expertise. His goal was to establish Republican political dominance at any cost.[4]

The next stage of totalitarian development is magical thinking or the open embrace of contradiction.

Trump failed to condemn the white supremacists who killed one and gravely injured dozens in Charlottesville. "We condemn in the strongest possible terms this egregious display of hatred, bigotry, and violence on many sides," Trump said.[5] He later read a statement calling racism evil. But the next day, he repeated his original "many sides" statement. Going forward, he retweeted misinformation from hate groups. His contradictions gave him cover with some and enabled him to be all things to all people.

The fourth state in the loss of truth and slide toward totalitarianism is blind faith in the leader. Truth is no longer based on fact, but on the assertions—true or not—of the leader.

At the end of World War II, a worker told Victor Klemperer, "Understanding is useless. You have to have faith. I believe in the Führer." President Trump told his followers, "I alone can fix it." Leaders on the Christian Right who speak of Trump as Jesus or King David are contributing to this kind of blind loyalty. To compare any leader to God is idolatrous. Trump has even called himself "the Chosen One." Using contradiction again, he said he was merely joking. In his book *Art of the Deal,* Trump advises:

> *Play to people's fantasies. People may not always think big themselves, but they can get*

> *very excited by those who do. That is why a*
> *little hyperbole never hurts. People want to be-*
> *lieve that something is the biggest, the greatest*
> *and the most spectacular.*[6]

Our modern media lends itself to spectacle, and Trump has spent a lifetime cultivating his ability to perform spectacle in partnership with those who pioneered it: Fox News's Roger Ailes, David Pecker of the *National Enquirer*, and even Trump's own reality-television show.

A LESSON FOR US

The truth is out there, but Americans must be more discerning than they have been willing to be of late. This environment is a real challenge for concerned pastors who tell me Fox News preaches to their flock 24/7 while they only have them a few hours a week at best.

The contradictions that permeate presidential and media messaging permit us to lie to ourselves and choose our own interpretation of the facts. Two days into Hitler's rule, German pastor and theologian Dietrich Bonhœffer, in a radio broadcast abruptly cut off ten minutes in, tried to warn German Christians not to embrace Hitler's promise of deliverance and redemption, rebirth and salvation. Bonhœffer soon began speaking of Hitler as the Antichrist to help people understand him as the "father of lies" masquerading as the savior of the German people.[7] His efforts bore little fruit as a majority of clergy and theologians pledged an oath of allegiance to Hitler.[8]

Thanks to the screens that are never far from our hands, we are tethered to negative stimuli and false narratives almost every waking moment. Even if we are not sucked into misinformation campaigns, the deluge of surreal headlines about gruesome murders, more gun violence, war, the climate crisis, corruption, and the latest attack tweet from the president leave us angry, anxious, dazed, and depressed. In this situation, it can be tempting to ask, "What is truth?" and wash our hands of the matter.

As long as our leadership obfuscates, redirects, and outright lies, we cannot rely on them to guide us. We must do our own investigation. We must do the work to discern the truth.

Modern Models: Restoring Balance and Alignment

Long before Pilate asked his question, Jesus answered it. In John 8:31–32, Jesus tells some of his followers, "If you continue in my word, you are truly my disciples; and you will know the truth, and the truth will make you free." Jesus told us his mission was to bring good news to the poor and freedom to the oppressed. *This* is the truth. If we continue to live out this truth, it will set us free. Embracing the idea that human beings could all live together in dignity and respect, free from tyranny, is what will make all of us free. Jesus' teachings can free us from the control of every tyrant's lies, propaganda, and desire to sow confusion.

For a democracy to survive, it requires objective, self-evident truths. How can we free ourselves from the tyrant's control to hear, see, and live these truths?

Many of us know that the claims President Trump makes about refugees being a threat to the nation are wrong because our congregations have been the primary institutions helping these families to resettle in this country. We should be creating such encounters locally, and many of us are doing so in powerful ways. In Columbus, Ohio, in 2016, clergy recognized the need to reignite a diverse coalition by examining racial equity within their meeting practices and their city. Black and white clergy began a monthly breakfast meeting, where they broke bread—or scrambled eggs—together.

The coalition grew quickly as leaders took seriously the need to become a more diverse body, meeting in different congregations—a mosque, a temple, and Black churches. This often meant getting outside their neighborhood as well as their comfort zone. Changing their meeting practices, which for many meant going into areas of the city they less often frequented, was a simple but big step. One white clergyman left saying that he'd never sat down with his fellow African-American clergy colleagues before.

But bigger than that, white clergy had to relinquish some of their desire to set the agenda. They had to talk about uncomfortable topics. Soon the group began to talk about racism in the city. When a twelve-year-old boy was shot by the police, the clergy were prepared to be challenged. Together they began to investigate police brutality. They discovered a truth hidden from everyone: Columbus had the highest per capita rate of police shootings of unarmed Black men in the nation.

After researching it further, clergy learned that the city had funding to implement best practices to curb the problem, but they had so far failed to do so. The group of clergy requested that the mayor (a Democrat) use the funds to implement a proven police-training program called Crisis Intervention Team. The clergy thought the request was logical and simple, yet it took sustained pressure over months and years to make headway. Along the way, they broadened the coalition to include concerned police, old-and-new-guard clergy, youth activists, and a diverse range of community groups and coalitions. Together they are making progress. They have had a number of successes, but they are also learning how entrenched power is in their city. It will take consistent effort to dethrone long-held, complex power structures driven by the status quo, greed, and self-interest. The coalition's earlier efforts to tweak certain policies are proving to be too small. The system itself is based on faulty assumptions and must be overhauled. A third of the Columbus City budget goes toward policing. Budgets are moral documents, and when we overinvest in policing, what are we saying? We are saying that God values punishment and surveillance over community, love, and care. As faith leaders, our moral responsibility is to push back on that narrative and ensure that every community has the resources they need. The clergy coalition in

Ohio continues to evolve and is now shifting efforts toward supporting Black leaders on the front lines of the movement who are imagining new ways of living together with safety and dignity. Eventually winning will require greater civic engagement around elections and a deeper vision of what is possible when we move from faith and not from fear.

HOW WE RESIST
Scripture has given us a number of spiritual disciplines designed to keep us from being enslaved to imperial cultural and political power.

First, keeping the Sabbath is one of the Ten Commandments. The idea of a day off in a world where slavery was unquestioned was an act of rebellion against an economy that exploited human labor. Observing the Sabbath enables us to resist the culture of empire by setting aside time to focus on the God who hears the cries of those in subjugation and on right relationships to others.

A rabbi friend mentioned to me that their Sabbath includes a weekend abstinence from screen time. People who are enslaved are not permitted to determine when they will take a break. Observing a Sabbath from screens—and the constant news cycle—is one way to let truth free us. Another goal of Sabbath in Abrahamic traditions is to restore balance. Perhaps in our congregations we can talk about balanced news consumption.

Second, faith communities provide opportunities for staying aligned with the God of Justice through ritual. I have been inspired by the Muslim ritual of praying five times a day facing Mecca. This practice provides multiple touch points throughout the day to reconnect with God and community. All day long, we are pelted with messages encouraging us to look a certain way, consume more, work harder, and ignore the needs of our bodies and souls. Anxiety is projected on news screens in many public locations. Our phones enable us to carry the world and its fear in our very pockets. Dings of news alerts sound even when we try to look away. Pausing to pray and meditate throughout the day is an act of resistance.

For Christians, the ritual of Communion can be a time where we take seriously the command to break bread together. The more we can use that to make eye contact, share, touch, use the senses, the more we will understand what Jesus gave us. We are enabled to remember that those who disagree with us politically are also family in Christ. It is a time to reflect on what it means for all to be welcome at the table, in the same way Jesus welcomed everyone regardless of status. Too often we make the ritual too efficient and individualistic. We sit in pews facing forward, eating "bread" that tastes like Styrofoam. Communion can be a liturgy of resistance—if we are willing to embrace it.

Third, our moral teachings free us to show compassion. This means our encounters with those suffering from oppression in our communities and around the world enable us to investigate for ourselves, to avoid black-and-white thinking, and to listen without dismissing others.

When Christians live in the way of that kingdom, or "kindom," as Ada Maria Isasi-Diaz has said, they are free, and no tyrant's lies can ever enslave God's children, whatever their race, religion, or nationality. To live in that way without being co-opted by tyrants requires that we know our Scripture as resistance literature and that we stay true to our spiritual disciplines. It also requires that we stay in touch with the lived realities of those the empire seeks to marginalize, examining these situations in the light of Scripture. Only then can we be certain of what is true.

Discussion Questions

1. Where do you primarily get your news? Why do you choose those sources? How do you prevent succumbing to disinformation and propaganda?
2. What are some rituals that help anchor you in a sea of information and misinformation?

CHAPTER 8
Reclaiming Our Voices

One has not only a legal but a moral responsibility to obey just laws. Conversely, one has a moral responsibility to disobey unjust laws.
—Rev. Dr. Martin Luther King Jr.

Romans 13 is one of the most abused texts in all of the Bible. Throughout centuries, the faithful have fought against this misappropriated chapter written by the apostle Paul to the Christian community in Rome that struggled against an emperor who claimed to be God and was threatened by claims that "Jesus is Lord/Caesar."

Anyone who tries to suggest that Scripture tells you to obey authorities in all circumstances is taking Scripture out of context. The Bible repeatedly calls on us in certain situations to disobey laws when they are unjust. Scripture is full of such examples. Paul spent lots of time in jail—not just for preaching that Jesus, not Caesar, is Lord, but for freeing people from economic captivity (Acts 16:16–40).

Making public scriptural arguments for what you want elected leaders to do is particularly critical when a misguided official explicitly justifies violations of human dignity using a religious or scriptural justification. We miss a valuable opportunity to debate our core values if we say such debates are off-limits. We can argue from our faith traditions while showing respect for ethical arguments—whatever their origin.

Our Past: The Slaves Who Ran to Freedom
The true story of Jane Johnson, a woman who fought her way to freedom in 1855 (based on her written testimony and news reports)

Just two months ago, I was a slave. The men who freed me were in jail. I am glad for my freedom, but it was hard to rest with these men in jail. A part of me was there with them.

My former master, Mr. Wheeler, was hell-bent on reclaiming "his property"—me and my two sons, Isaiah and Daniel. I learned from my new friend Mrs. Lucretia Mott that the Fugitive Slave Act allowed liberated slaves to be hunted down even in free states. It also allowed for the jailing of those who came to their aid. Judge Kane, of the District Court of the United States for the Eastern District of Pennsylvania, had held Mr. Williamson on "contempt of court" for refusing to reveal my whereabouts, and they would not free him until the "property" was returned.

Before we left Washington, Mr. Wheeler's family had warned him about passing through Philadelphia on his way to New York City, then onto Nicaragua, where Mr. Wheeler would serve as ambassador. "They are a bunch of lawbreaking, godless thugs there, John! How do you know Jane won't run?"

He had chuckled, confidently waving away their concerns and looking at me with condescension, claiming the Fugitive Slave Act protected him. "Besides," he continued, "Jane is a Christian. She knows slaves must submit to their masters and we Christians must uphold the laws, for God has ordained them." He looked at me and nodded as though we shared a faith and a common understanding.

I kept my face calm as though I agreed. *But God broke the laws of tyrants and freed slaves,* I reminded myself.

That night I had packed a suit to use as a disguise to escape when we got to New York. I had my children, Isaiah and Daniel, in tow.

My opportunity to escape came sooner than New York City, thanks to Mr. Still, the colored man who clerked for the Pennsylvania Society for Promoting the Abolition of Slavery, and Mr. Passmore Williamson, a white man who was a Quaker Christian,[1] alongside Isaiah, William, John, and James, helped me flee Mr. Wheeler. All of these men had been jailed on charges of rioting, assault, and battery. Mr. Wheeler claimed they violently kidnapped me and my two children.

So now I was back at the courthouse in Philadelphia, the belly of the beast. I had to set the record straight. As we arrived, I saw the steps were full of protesters, police, and reporters. The Society had been organizing protests. All the papers were telling our story. I walked up the stone courthouse steps with my female companions who worked to free slaves.

We sat in the courtroom silently waiting for the crowds to settle and the trial to start. I had time to collect my thoughts, remembering everything that happened that day. My thoughts were interrupted as Judge Kane walked in from his chambers in the front: "All Rise!" It might have been my imagination, but he looked rattled. The city was in an uproar that the judge put Mr. Williamson in jail like that, with no trial, no jury. I bet he was feeling the pressure. My former master might be friends with the president, but the Society had public opinion on its side.

Passmore Williamson was brought in. He looked worn—two months in one of the worst jails in the country would do that to you, I'm sure—but determined.

"Your Honor," said our attorney, "I call Jane Johnson to the stand."

I threw back the veil I was wearing to hide my identity, and I heard gasps and murmurings from the gallery. The Judge tapped his gavel and called for order.

I told him how I boarded the boat in Philadelphia and saw a colored man and a white one. The white man beckoned me to come to him, and the colored man closer to me asked, "Do you desire your freedom?" I said, "Yes, I do, and I always have."

WHO STOLE **MY BIBLE?**

The white man then approached Mr. Wheeler and said he desired to tell him my rights. Mr. Wheeler said, "My woman knows her rights." He tried to stop me.

But the white man, Mr. Passmore Williamson, held out his hand and I rose to go with him. I took my oldest boy by the hand and someone picked up my youngest. I left the boat as quickly as I could, being perfectly willing and desirous to go.

At that, it seemed all the color went out of Judge Kane's face. He was still, like the calm before a storm. He looked over at the reporters, who were scribbling furiously.

"That will be all, Your Honor," said the lawyer for Mr. Williamson.

I was weak with relief. I felt people around me ushering me out of the courtroom. Suddenly outside, I was surrounded by a flank of officers. I was frightened, but Mrs. Mott told me these were Pennsylvania officers there to protect me from federal officers. A carriage pulled up, the horses snorting with excitement as though they could sense danger. Once in the carriage with Mrs. Mott, we galloped away at breakneck speed.

As we sped away, I saw Lucretia's face lit up with excitement. She looked at me with tears in her eyes, "Miss Jane, you courageous woman, you! You have started a revolution. The nation will never be the same."

UNDERSTANDING THE TEXT

In 1806, missionaries sent to the colony of Barbados brought with them a Bible called *Parts of the Holy Bible, selected for the use of the Negro Slaves, in the British West-India Islands*. The Slave Bible, as it is commonly known, was published three years after the Haitian Revolution freed slaves.

To create a Bible that was safe to teach to slaves, the editors of the Slave Bible removed 90 percent of the Hebrew Bible. The Slave Bible excised the story of Moses leading the Israelites to freedom, but included Joseph's enslavement in Egypt. Sermons aimed at enslaved people portrayed Joseph as someone who accepted his lot in life, kept his faith in God, and in the end was rewarded for it.

They also removed half of the New Testament. Among the excluded passages are Galatians 3:28: "There is neither Jew nor Greek, there is neither bond nor free, there is neither male nor female: for ye are all one in Christ Jesus," which was thought to incite rebellion.

The two passages they made sure to include and emphasize were Romans 13 and Ephesians 6:5, which states, "Servants, be obedient to them that are your masters according to the flesh, with fear and trembling, in singleness of your heart, as unto Christ."

The Bible was a radical document that threatened the institution of slavery. It had to be controlled.

Debates around Romans 13 grew during the early 1800s and peaked just before the Civil War. In one response to pro-slavery biblical argumentation published in the *Vermont Telegraph* in 1840, an abolitionist argued that this notion that Christians should submit to governing authorities regardless of what leaders do is an "outrage against common sense." He wrote, "According to this doctrine, Pharaoh, Nero, Caligula, Domitian, Alexander, Napoleon and every wholesale murderer who has flooded the earth with human gore has been an approved servant of God!"

The chapter headings of Romans, he explained, were not assigned by Paul, but by a later editor. The division of Romans into chapters 12 and 13 breaks the subject artificially and interrupts Paul's argument. These two chapters should be examined as one.

Cherice Bock, in her recent work "Quakers' Relation to the State," likewise demonstrates that Romans 12:17 through 13:10 are part of one narrative that centers on the theme of love: how Christians express love within and outside the Christian community.[2] "The overall point of the long passage is to call believers to remain firmly grounded in God's goodness while interacting with the world around them in peace and love."[3]

WHO STOLE **MY BIBLE?**

Toward the end of Chapter 12, Paul begins to expand the circle of love beyond family, other believers, and community to how believers treat their enemies. They are to show love even to those who persecute them. This passage is the basis for centuries-old teachings on pacifism and nonviolent resistance. Paul then moves from this expansion of the love ethic to the larger circle of how Christians are to relate to the state. When understood as part of a progression of ideas Paul is laying out, the first seven verses of Chapter 13 logically flow from the ethic of love being expanded from enemies and even to the state itself. But what does that look like?

Nowhere else in the Bible is the phrase "be subject to" translated as "obey."[4] The authorities elsewhere in the Bible translate it as "participate in the order of." This matches a Jewish understanding that God places rulers in power, we should be part of their ordering of society, but that does not mean they must always be obeyed, as seen in stories from the Babylonian exile (Daniel, Shadrach, Meshach, and Abednego, for instance).

The grammar of the phrase in verse 6, translated as "for the authorities are God's servants, busy with this very thing," would be more accurately translated, "they are God's servants only to the extent they are busy doing this very thing."[5] Christians give the authorities the respect they are owed only to the extent that the authorities are acting in appropriate ways in the first place.

America Today: Using the Bible to Deny Freedom

United States Attorney General Jeff Sessions was standing before an audience of law enforcement officials in Fort Wayne, Indiana.

He was under fire from all quarters for his "Zero Tolerance" immigration policy that mandated border officials separate migrant children from their moms and dads who were, in most cases, fleeing violence and seeking asylum in America. Reports emerged that the administration had separated at least 650 children—even toddlers and infants—from their parents. Horrifyingly, they had even lost track of many of them. Tape recordings surfaced that captured the voices of children crying "Mommy!" while guards teased. The nation was horrified. Attorney General Sessions was unmoved.

The eyes of the world were on the attorney general. But rather than speak the language of law enforcement, Sessions surprisingly turned to the Bible.

"I would like to cite to you the Apostle Paul and his clear and wise command in Romans 13. The Bible argues Christians must 'obey the laws of the government because God has ordained them for the purpose of order.'"

Later, Sarah Huckabee Sanders, the White House press secretary, summed up the same idea: "It is very biblical to enforce the law."

A LESSON FOR US

The Trump administration very publicly rebuked the faith community for morally condemning this ungodly policy of child separation. The attorney general was not just speaking to an audience of law enforcement officials that day in Indiana. He used the news cameras to speak to every Christian in the country. And he told us to shut up and obey the government because our God-ordained duty is to obey governments—no matter what they do.

That an attorney general would use Scripture to tell us to tolerate human suffering is sickening. But it is also good news. His need to rebuke us revealed that our moral voice was a threat to the imperial reality—to the reality that a tyrannical administration was trying to shape.

So often I have been in circles that have doubted the power of their moral voice to effect change. After years of seeing Scripture misrepresented, we have grown ashamed of our public voice. Some of us have even rejected the power of Scripture. This moment in history should help us see the power our Scripture holds both for our own inspiration and to stop tyrants in their tracks.

Modern Models: Reclaiming Our Voice

The response from the faith community resounded throughout the nation. Progressive activist groups and denominations alike rushed in to condemn the argument and the undergirding policy. Conservative traditions also spoke out, including the Southern Baptist Convention and the Church of Jesus Christ of Latter-day Saints. Even some of Trump's own religious allies who had rarely, if ever, criticized him made their discomfort known. Using more than just words, religious leaders rushed to the border to expose the severity of what was happening, to bear witness to the suffering.

We said in one voice, "No!" Scripture tells us to welcome the stranger and to oppose the government when it deviates from our values. Jack Jenkins, one of the top religion reporters in the country, said, "Sessions's attempt at theological debate quickly became one of the biggest embarrassments of Trump's young administration. . . . It was, without question, the single most uniform theological denunciation of a policy I have ever encountered as a religion journalist."[6]

All social change starts with imagination. A people who can imagine that the world can be different is a people that cannot, will not, be controlled. This is why slaveholders sought to control slave religion and the Bible. This is why Sessions reverted to slaveholding arguments in his defense of child separation.

Our voices matter. We cannot, will not, cede the language of faith. I have met many who do not want to speak specifically from Scripture because they worry it will offend other faiths or might cross a line between "separation of Church and State." I believe we can weigh in specifically from our own faith tradition and holy texts while showing respect for other traditions. We can welcome those of all faiths and no faith, while sharing how we look at a particular issue. In doing so, we model civil dialogue and respect—critical characteristics of public speech in a democracy—as well as bring the wisdom of our traditions to bear on important policy debates. Most often, I have found people relieved, grateful, and curious to hear more. I often have run across folks disaffected from faith who consider reconnecting to their religious tradition after seeing our message of faith and justice.

What if no one had pushed back on Attorney General Jeff Sessions's misrepresentation of Scripture and exposed the history of this abusive text? His moral assertions would have further confused those whose consciences might otherwise have been piqued. He might have taken the moral high ground. I believe some of the reason voices of intolerance and injustice have gained so much ground is that many of us mistakenly shied away from using our faith voice, choosing to get involved and speak out, but not from the angle of our religious belief.

HOW WE RESIST

Throughout history and in Scripture, people of faith have broken laws that are unjust. God calls us to uphold just laws, but to break unjust laws that violate God's command to love one another as we would love ourselves.

The religious community's public theological debate with the attorney general shows how our moral and theological resources are critical to preserving our democracy, as is our willingness to disobey laws not grounded by the ethic of love. Standing up to an unjust judge—or attorney general, as the case may be—is an article of faith.

For many of us, this will mean gaining confidence in our knowledge of biblical texts and theological thought. Sometimes we know the two are connected, but we haven't taken time to think it through. I once met a young Methodist woman working for a premier women's rights organization. She saw me helping to lead a multifaith coalition of women at the United Nations and asked, "How are you doing this? At church I cannot talk about my work; and at work I cannot talk about my faith." I gave her a stack of feminist and womanist theology texts. She came back the next month and told me, "I have been talking about this everywhere! My husband cautioned me that I might offend someone at church or work. But I told him I cannot stop. It is such good news!" She was so energized about her new discovery. It fueled her faith journey and her work.

Strengthen those muscles! You need not be a pastor or have a seminary education to do this work.

You might also begin to think about ways to get your voice out there. If you like to write, consider writing Letters to the Editor or an opinion piece for your local paper. If you have something to say, but are not a writer, hire someone or find a volunteer to do so. Find others who would join you in speaking out. And reach out for support to the growing network of progressive faith organizations.

Bringing our faith voice to the public square can be a deeply worshipful experience. I think of this as a spiritual discipline as well. I'm following in the footsteps of Moses, Miriam, Mary, and the prophets. I have never felt closer to God than at those times when I am at a rally lifting up God's vision of liberation. It is no wonder it feels like worship. For one thing, the Hebrew word for worship means "to serve." It makes sense that serving the community would feel worshipful—perhaps it is the purist form of worship. When I have joined press conferences, every single faith leader, whatever their faith, has preached to my soul. I have come to think of press conferences as a type of revival (and you can enjoy some of them on our Facebook page at Faith in Public Life). We are proclaiming the good news in word, in action, in solidarity, and in song. It is then that I most feel the spirit moving in my life and in the community.

Discussion Questions
1. What were you taught about obedience to authorities growing up? Do you agree with the author that Scripture teaches us to only obey laws rooted in love? Why?

2. Do you feel like your faith voice matters and that your voice matters? Why? What "muscles" do you need to exercise, in able to speak out with a voice grounded in Scripture?

CHAPTER 9
Witnessing to the Liberative Power of God

Hope is an embrace of the unknown and the unknowable, an alternative to the certainty of both optimists and the pessimists. . . . It's the belief that what we do matters even though how and when it may matter, who and what it may impact, are not things we can know beforehand. . . . History is full of people whose influence was most powerful after they were gone.
—Rebecca Solnit

The Antichrist. The Battle of Armageddon. The dreaded Four Horsemen of the Apocalypse.

You don't have to have read the Bible or gone to church to know about the Book of Revelation. It is undoubtedly the most well-known book in the Bible, but also the least understood. Revelation even baffles biblical scholars and vexed early Church leaders who debated whether or not to include it in the canon.

American interpretations of Revelation have been more defined by a combination of Hollywood storytelling and modern politics than anything else, much to our detriment. Movies and political rhetoric don't always make good theology.

Today 40 to 60 percent of contemporary Americans embrace key elements of a Revelation-based end-times scenario known as "premillennial dispensationalism"—an eschatological system formulated in the mid-nineteenth century by the British churchman John Darby.[1] Darby taught that there would be millennium in the future, a golden age, where Christ reigns on Earth. Christ would return and defeat evil, after a tribulation marked by natural disasters and wars, and an Antichrist, as the Book of Revelation notes. At the end of that period, the people of the Mosaic covenant, including the Jews, would convert.

In 1970, Hal Lindsey's bestseller *The Late Great Planet Earth* popularized a kind of dispensationalism and was turned into a blockbuster documentary.[2] The *Left Behind* series of Tim LaHaye and Jerry Jenkins published in the 1990s is a fictionalized treatment of Darby's system. It racked up sales of more than 60 million copies.

In Lindsey's book, one of the harbingers of the end times include the return of Jews to the Holy Land (founding of Israel in 1948); Jews regaining control of Jerusalem's sacred sites (the 1967 Arab-Israeli War); and the rebuilding of the Temple (not yet, but Google this, combined with Trump, and you can see people are already conjecturing). When the apocalypse comes, Jews would either repent or go to Hell. Such views are a great source of antisemitism. At the same time, the belief that the restoration of Israel and building of the Temple will bring about Christ's return have led white evangelicals to give their unquestioning loyalty to Israel, often at great expense to human rights in the region.

These titillating interpretations have unfortunately led to some damaging political views that do untold harm. According to LaHaye and Lindsey, the Antichrist would return as a man of peace settling the Israeli-Palestinian conflict. This led both fiction writers to depict the UN secretary-general as the Antichrist, since UN efforts at peacemaking between Israel and Palestine would be disruptive to "God's plan." As one of the founders of the Christian Right, LaHaye deeply opposed the United Nations' focus on the rights of women, children, and LGBTQ people.[3] The UN's focus on international cooperation runs counter to LaHaye's and other Christian Right leaders' nationalistic, America

First worldview. Their opposition to the UN's peacemaking and human rights work hampered efforts to address conflicts in the Middle East, fueled efforts to defund UN development and peacekeeping agencies, and damaged the health, well-being, and safety of women, children, and LGBTQ people globally.

Dispensationalism has impacted white Christian views of President Trump as well. In *God's Man in the White House*, professor James Beverley documents a comprehensive collection of over 500 prophecies about Trump, covering a period of fifteen years, by more than 100 of the leading Christian prophets and leaders in the USA and worldwide, providing the political and religious context for the ongoing prophecies and controversies about the 45th president of the USA.[4]

Ironically, these theories have led Christians to embrace the very anti-Jesus imperial-domination systems the author of Revelation rejected.

Thank God John's audience did not read this letter for those who would live two millennia later. Had they considered it a prediction for others, John's dire message would have fallen on deaf ears! By reading Revelation with new eyes, we can reclaim John's vision for how to live faithfully in a world where living out your values is increasingly difficult, and where the future—with our capacity to shape it—looks bleak.

Our Past: A Dire Revelation

I sat in the darkness. There was no moon out. With the darkness pressing in around me, my sense of isolation on the small rocky island of Patmos grew so intense I found it hard to breathe. I was wired, and despite a full day of working the mines, I was not ready to sleep.

I looked to the stars that burned brightly with the lack of moon. I could not see the craggy rocks on the island, so I let my vision float out beyond the heavens. Then I began to pray, first giving God thanks for the Jesus followers of the seven cities I had tended to before Rome exiled me to this tiny rock in the Aegean.

Ephesus, with its patient endurance; Pergamum, faithful even under persecution of Herod Antipas; and Thyatira, committed to acts of compassion and service.

Once I had given thanks for all the churches, I lifted up my fears and anxieties. Smyrna was impoverished by landgrabs by the elite and heavy taxation, belittled because of their beliefs. Would they stay strong? Pergamum had been tempted by the teaching of the Nicolaitans to accommodate Rome. Would their previous courage and resistance endure? Lamb of God, give them strength!

Lord, how I missed the freedom to travel to the seven cities! Even now, my spirit could at least wander there in prayer. If only I could get word to them. But to do so would be dangerous for me and for them.

Upon finishing this petitionary prayer, I tried to empty my mind and simply listen, breathing deeply and slowly.

My mind drifted to the altercation that landed me in this speck of craggy land in the vast Aegean Sea. I saw myself in the Temple, challenging the authorities for extracting more denarii from a poor peasant who hoped merely to get a "mark" from temple authorities so he could buy bread for his family. Even now, I burned with righteous anger, wondering about the poor farmer's fate. It had been the last straw for the Roman authorities. They already knew of my disdain for the emperor and of my travels to the seven churches.

My wife told me that the stories of Christ followers would be the death of us both. As a Jew, I was already suspect. In that moment in the Temple, I had felt like Moses, intervening when an Egyptian beat a poor Hebrew man. I felt like Jesus overturning tables in the Temple. In that moment, as the poor man wept and pled for his children, something in me snapped. I acted.

The years had been hard for all of us. First the Jewish Revolt in 66 CE. Then the destruction of the Temple. Thousands had been killed and thousands more paraded as slaves through

Rome, and the treasures of Jerusalem were used to build Rome's Coliseum. Then came the deranged emperor Nero, the one they called 666. He had burned many of my friends alive. It was rumored he was still alive and would return from the East and take power.

The trauma of these events left many in despair. My wife was deeply shaken. Could she hold up without me? I agonized over whether or not I had done the right thing that day. Would my actions bear fruit? Or had they been for naught? Would the peasant be better off, or would he and my churches now face persecution? Was God in any of this? Had I been faithful or foolish?

New images and symbols swam before me as I let my vision drift deep into the stars. I felt as though I was no longer sitting on the rock, but instead drifting into the heavens. The Roman soldier who had arrested me flashed before my eyes. His face morphed to the face of Emperor Domitian. This face, ubiquitous on coinage and buildings, became a beast with seven horns. Good God! Behind the beast was a dragon. Satan!

Now came a lamb who roared like a lion. The lamb became a rider with a sword coming from his mouth and diadems on his head (Rev. 21:1): "Be my witness," said the lamb. "I am your fellow servant with you and your comrades who will hold the witness of Jesus . . . the spirit of prophecy. Behold, there will be a new Heaven and a new earth!"

When I woke, I knew somehow, I would have to get word to the churches. My people were in danger. They would need to be strengthened and prepared to resist what was coming so they could remain faithful and true to the word of God. Come what may, they must be witnesses that Jesus, not Caesar, is Lord.

UNDERSTANDING THE TEXT
John of Patmos calls the contents of his letter an *Apokalypsis*, or revelation, about "what must soon take place." This sense of urgency is repeated throughout the letter. His vision is

an urgent matter for his community: the Seven Churches of Ephesus, Smyrna, Pergamum, Thyatira, Sardis, Philadelphia, and Laodicea.

As explored in the chapter on Pontius Pilate, John wrote during an era where the imperial cult—emperor worship— increasingly dominated all aspects of life. John of Patmos lived under the Emperor Domitian, who actually commissioned a choir to follow him everywhere he went, singing, "You are worthy, our lord and god, to receive honor and glory and power."

So when John begins by asserting that Jesus, not Domitian, was "the ruler of the kings of the earth" (Rev. 1:5), he is reminding his readers that Jesus is Lord and God, and Jesus alone deserves honor and glory.

It was impossible to participate in any aspect of Roman life without being part of the imperial cult. With military might and the threat of crucifixion, Rome forced conquered nations to submit to emperor worship. All commerce transpired at Roman temples and subjects had to receive a "mark," showing that they had paid tribute and made a sacrifice to Caesar as the Lord. To eat, one had to bow to Caesar. When John wrote that "no one can buy or sell" without the "mark of the beast" (Rev. 13:16-17), he meant it.[5]

As the Roman Empire expanded and consolidated, it brought about inequality and misery. It consolidated small, subsistence family farms into large agribusiness, pushing families off their land to work at low wages in urban areas. Over 99 percent of its population lived in abject poverty. The historian Appian wrote: "The rich had got possession of the greater part of the undivided land. . . . Thus the powerful men drew all wealth to themselves, and all the land swarmed with slaves."[6]

The political class consisted largely of these landowners, but many elites made money from trade in luxury goods, such as those listed in Revelation 18:12-13, goods that could bring in high profits. The imposition of taxes to fund endless wars, and the transition to a money rather than bartering economy, led to debt, bondage, and slavery for many under Roman rule.

John reveals the spiritual truth behind this brutal system using a number of symbols. We may never know exactly the meaning of all of these, but a number seem clear from historical research.

God's opponents are represented by four symbols in John's vision: the Dragon, the Beast from the Sea, the Beast from the Earth, and Babylon. Satan is the Dragon (Rev. 12:9) and he controls these other beasts that seem to represent aspects of Rome's imperial power.

The sea beast is Rome's military power—it invades from the sea. The Beast of the Sea (Rev. 13:1-10) is a combination of the four beasts in the Book of Daniel (Chap. 7), which is John's way of saying that Rome is more powerful than all past empires combined.

The Beast from the Earth (Rev. 13:11) represents Rome's cultic power. This beast creates an image of the beast and threatens to execute those who refuse to worship its image (13:15). This beast makes everyone wear the "mark" so they can buy and sell.

The third enemy, the whore of Babylon, represents the economic and cultural power of Rome (Rev. 18:3b): "All the merchants of the earth have grown rich from the power of her luxury." In 17:4-6, her wealth and beauty in gold and pearls are described. The chapter describes the wealth and goods made possible by empire—gold, ivory, fine linens, spice, incense, myrrh, wine, and much more. It ends on a chilling note about how the wealth is produced (18:12-13): "horses and chariots, slaves, and human lives."

The web of association among the Dragon, the Beast from the Sea, the Beast from the Earth, Babylon, and the inhabitants of the earth make up the system of imperial domination. Rome is evil, and those who collaborate with Rome are to be part of the imperial system.

John shows Rome's true nature, and in doing so, forces

a stark moral choice on his people. They may be drawn to Rome's splendor, but it is rotten and satanic underneath.

Standing against this titillating, yet exploitative, beast, whom no one can oppose (13:4), stands Jesus the Lamb, who is a witness to the word of God.

Some have erroneously translated the letters of the Greek word *martys* into their corresponding roman letters as "martyr." The accurate translation is the legal term *witness.*[7]

John says in Revelation 1:5 that Jesus is the prime witness who testified to God's truth, even at the cost of his own life. He connects the witness of Jesus to the word of God, which is this: "Christ is Lord." John is asking his flock to bear witness to the fact that Jesus, not Domitian, is Lord. To do so, they must resist the entire cultic, military, and economic system (the two beasts and Babylon) by living out Jesus' word.

The goal is not martyrdom or suffering in and of itself, as some have emphasized, often to the detriment of those already living under oppressive systems. The goal is resistance, which may lead to suffering, even death. But in the end, God will have the last word.

Jesus is revealed to John first as a Lion of the tribe of Judah (Rev. 5:5). The lion then becomes a lamb "standing as if it had been slaughtered, having seven horns and seven eyes" (Rev. 5:6). This Jesus is a powerful, conquering, slaughtered Lion-Lamb throughout Revelation (5:5–6, 6; 12:11; 17:14). What a mixed metaphor!

This Lion-Lamb (5:5–6) mounts a warhorse to do battle with the beast (19:11–16). In 19:15, "His name is called The Word of God. . . . From his mouth comes a sharp sword with which to strike down the nations." The sword is not in his hand, but in his mouth, representing the word. The Word-Sword cuts against the contrary witness that Rome and Caesar are Lord.

Again, Jesus' word—think of the Sermon on the Mount and in parables, as well as his ministry, healing, teaching, and exorcisms—was a counter to the assertion that Caesar was the

Lord. Despite appearances, Jesus is Lord and his good news, or imperial decree (*evangelion*), is that those who are impoverished and thrown in debtors' prisons will be set free (Luke 4:18-19).

John asks his followers to be *martys*/witnesses. Before Jesus rides out, John falls down at his feet to worship him, but Jesus says (19:10), "You must not do that! I am a fellow servant with you and your comrades who hold the witness of Jesus. Worship God! For the testimony of Jesus is the spirit of prophecy." We are all to witness, as Jesus did, to the spirit of prophecy. Repeatedly, John returns to the idea that all who follow Jesus are priests, as first announced at Sinai.

Suffering is not the goal, but it is sometimes the result of witnessing. "When Jesus mounts his horse, it is to change the world, not suffer for it." Womanist theologian Delores Williams argues that the cross and Jesus' crucifixion upon it "are reminders of what can happen to reformers who successfully challenge the status quo and try to bring about a new dispensation of love and power for the poor."[8]

The witness of the Lamb is not unlike the witness of Martin Luther King Jr., says New Testament scholar Brian Blount. "[King], like the Lamb, deployed nonviolent resistance, drawing out the reactionary violence of racial injustice and transforming it."[9] The students who stood firm at lunch counters and witnessed to a truth contrary to white supremacy were following the Lamb with the sword in its mouth who conquers with the word of Faithfulness and Truth.

John is telling Christians to "come out of the closet" and witness to the word of justice in the face of a brutal empire asserting its control. They are to resist the temptation to go with the flow of the imperial economic, cultic, and military status quo. In standing out, they would undoubtedly face persecution, as John had.

The reward would be great, for, in time, God would cast aside the empires of the world. God would create a "new Heaven and new earth," where "death will be no more, mourning and crying and pain will be no more." In Revelation 21:1-7, God tells them to look beyond their current reality of suffering and injustice and "See I am making all things new."

America Today: Revelation Redux
In Revelation 13:4, one of John's most poignant observations is that when the people saw the Beast of the Sea, they worshiped it, saying: "Who is like the beast and who can fight against it?"

So often, the oppressive and dysfunctional systems we are up against seem unchangeable and unassailable. Resistance seems futile. Rome certainly drove this point home through horrific public crucifixions and symbols of imperial power on every corner.

The Jewish uprising that led to the destruction of the Jerusalem Temple just a few years prior had proved this point: no one could escape or defend against the beast of Rome. Catastrophe had befallen Israel and now Jews, among them Christ following Jews, were on the run. Rome had a totalitarian lockdown on all aspects of life. John himself was sitting in prison on Patmos, uncertain of his own fate.

Today we are suffering through a series of catastrophes: a 2008 economic collapse that we claim to have recovered from, but it left behind many Americans; a pandemic that has taken nearly 200,000 lives (as of this writing), and surely will claim as many more; an economic collapse caused by the president's failure to heed advice from medical experts; a racial justice uprising whose demands have yet to be realized, despite the embrace of the slogan "Black Lives Matter"; a nascent democracy whose institutions are now teetering on the brink of collapse; a planet threatened by climate change while our nation rolls back regulations and treaties to arrest ecological devastation.

John would say that these catastrophes are an apocalypse—not the end of the world, but a revelation—should we allow ourselves to see it—of the greedy, bloodthirsty imperial beast beneath the fine linens and glittering jewels. Though unwelcome, these crises are an opportunity to see and do something new. The many-headed beasts reveal the corruption of the imperial system around us. The imperial cult of the United States of America, whose stock market booms while unemployment skyrockets, had numbed many of us to our own reality. The pandemic itself pulls back the veil showing us that we can no longer permit a health care system that fails to cover all of us. The murder of George Floyd reveals to us that resources are being siphoned out of community development and into militarizing our police; and it shows us that Jim Crow—never fully dismantled—reasserted its power by dismantling voting rights and resegregating schools.

A LESSON FOR US

Like the people of Rome, we might be tempted to succumb to the power of the beast, either by accommodating or by curling up in despair. It would be easy for us to doubt whether our nonviolent, lamblike faith can go up against a slaughtering beast and win. Is the revolutionary love we speak of strong enough to challenge all of this? Do our votes count? Does our organizing ever pay off?

John, writing from a penal colony, said yes. He encouraged his followers to choose a different state of mind and to invest in the goodness of God, even at the risk of death, even though success seemed unlikely.

Throughout history, leaders of justice movements have asserted the same claim. Václav Havel, a dissident during the Cold War, wrote from a Soviet prison: "Hope is the ability to work for something because it is good, not because it stands a chance to succeed." The political dissident, who had every reason to doubt whether his life of daring and sacrifice would pay off, said, "Hope is a state of mind, not a state of the world."

Modern Models: Struggling for Hope

Austin Channing Brown speaks of this kind of hope in her book *I'm Still Here: Black Dignity in a World Made for Whiteness*. She writes that, given the persistence of racism in America, "hope for me has died one thousand deaths." She continues, "I have learned not to fear the death of hope. . . . I have come to rest in the *shadow of hope*." The shadow of hope is in "knowing that we may never see the realization of our dreams and yet still showing up."[10]

By way of example, Channing Brown quotes Ta-Nehisi Coates who, when asked if he hoped racism in American would somehow change, said, "Slavery in this country was 250 years."[11] This means, he continued, that there were people born in this country in 1750 who, if they looked backward, saw their parents were slaves, as were their grandparents and their great-grandparents. And if they look forward, their children would be slaves as well as their grandchildren and possibly their great-grandchildren.

There was no real hope and yet they struggled, and they resisted.

In *Bury the Chains*, Adam Hochschild tells how a handful of hopefuls gathered in a London print shop in 1785 to organize the movement that in half a century helped abolish slavery in the British Empire.[12] The International Criminal Court, first proposed in 1919 but shelved during the Cold War, was resurrected by a small band of human rights activists working through an obscure UN committee that managed to move the idea forward in 1989 before the world's superpower could stop it. In July 2013, the acquittal of George Zimmerman in the shooting death of African-American teen Trayvon Martin gave birth to the slogan "Black Lives Matter"—an assertion then considered radical, even offensive. Today it is embraced by the mainstream, thanks to persistent organizing of Black-led organizations that built a "leader-full" movement based on shared power.

No idea worth fighting for ever looked possible. And most

visions take generations to realize, and subsequent generations to protect and refine them.

HOW WE RESIST

John encourages his followers to be watchful, to see the corruption and depravity that lurks behind the glamour, to note the weakness in the underbelly of the brute, to see ourselves as comrades of the Lion-Lamb. John and his people could have fallen into despair. They could have chosen to be drawn into the imperial culture. As an antidote, John gives them clarity about what is at stake. They have a choice. They can give in or they can show up.

For John, showing up means to witness to the goodness of God in the liberating Christ, to be Jesus' comrades, even when that means becoming outcasts and putting ourselves at odds with brutal empires. I can imagine Jesus' followers refusing the "mark" and instead establishing their own sharing economy, like the early believers in Acts who shared everything in common (Acts 2:42). It could have meant refusing to allow their children to be conscripted into military service. Maybe it meant resisting the temptation to seek social and political power by selling out to Caesar.

To witness is to show up, not knowing the outcome. To be faithful is to act and leave the results to God who promises a new Heaven and a new earth. John tells his people that things may get worse before they get better. Some may die before this is over. John assures them that God, in the form of a nonviolent lamb who lifts up a vision of a new earth, is powerful enough to take on the beast, who threatens violence, poverty, and spiritual captivity.

In this time of daunting challenges, faith communities are proposing bold agendas. Given the challenges, some might be tempted to just "do the best we can." We might feel we need to temper our asks of our leaders and be realistic. But that is not the vision John had in Revelation, nor does it match up with the heroes of the Bible who countered brutal empires with a radical love ethic. It's time to go big or go home.

The preamble to the Moral Policy Poor People's Campaign platform is an example of Revelation-style hope:

> *The evils of systemic racism, poverty, ecological devastation, and the war economy and militarism are persistent, pervasive, and perpetuated by a distorted moral narrative that must be challenged.*

> *We must stop the attention violence that refuses to see these injustices and acknowledge the human and economic costs of inequality. We believe that when decent people see the faces and facts . . . they will be moved deeply in their conscience to change things. When confronted with the undeniable truth of unconscionable cruelty to our fellow human beings, we must join the ranks of those who are determined not to rest until justice and equality are a reality for all.*

So, too, the preamble of Faith in Public Life reads:

> *The 2020 election is a referendum on the values that will shape our future.*

> *Many of the defining moral issues of our time are on the ballot: faltering democratic institutions, extreme inequality of wealth and power, the existential threat of climate change, cruel immigration policies that tear apart families, mass incarceration that devastates communities of color, senseless gun violence,*

and threats to global public health and security.

These challenges are daunting. We must move forward in a spirit of hope, and resist despair and cynicism.

For generations, people of faith have been at the forefront of struggles for justice, leading seemingly unwinnable movements. From the abolition of slavery to women's suffrage and the civil rights movement, religious activists have proven that faith and action are powerful catalysts for social change.

The challenges we confront today require us to envision who we wish to be as a nation. Appeals to nationalism put a new face on the sin of white supremacy. People of color and members of Jewish, Muslim, Sikh, Hindi and other faith traditions are too often targeted by dehumanizing rhetoric and racist policies. When we resist this culture of exclusion, we affirm that all of us are created in the sacred image of God.

From the elections of 2020 and for years to come, communities of faith will hold whatever party is in power accountable to these demands. We do not know exactly when or how, or if, these demands will be realized. But our hope is in God making all things new. And it is a great joy—even when times are tough—to be comrades with Jesus in this new thing.

Discussion Questions
1. America is an empire. Where do you see attributes of the Roman imperial cult active in America today?

2. Where do you see yourself and those around you accommodating empire?
3. What does witness look like to you? What gives you hope in these times to continue working for a better country and world? How does your faith strengthen you?

CONCLUSION

Days before he would succumb to cancer, Civil Rights icon and Georgia congressman, John Lewis, made his way to the newly painted Black Lives Matter Plaza in front of the White House to "see and feel for myself . . . how truth is still marching on."[1] He came away with a glimpse of the Promised Land reflected in the faces of racial justice leaders protesting the murder of George Floyd, Breonna Taylor, Ahmaud Arbery, and countless others.

No one would have blamed John Lewis if he had thrown up his hands in despair. Instead, this man who had risked his own life multiple times to end Jim Crow segregation, this man who watched many of those gains reversed, spent his final breaths and steps celebrating a younger generation that would bring his accomplishments forward. John Lewis saw great possibility as millions of young people took to the streets. They carried pain and lament, but they also came to bear witness to the world they hoped to birth. The pounding of many youthful feet laid straight a path through the wilderness, and John Lewis had faith that they would bring us to the Promised Land. His hope persisted through all of it.

The author of Hebrews urged his flock as they faced daunting hurdles to look both forward and back for the long lineage of biblical heroes (Heb. 11:13): "Died in faith without having received the promises, but from a distance they saw and greeted them."

We often do not see in our lifetime the total fruits of our labor. Ours is to witness, not knowing if we will live to see the day when our "work pays off." We are free to be participants in God's plan and let go of the rest, trusting God will bring it to fruition.

As a can-do person, I will admit to chafing sometimes at this. I feel my American bootstrap cultural upbringing screaming from the depths, "I will make my own destiny!" I feel my do-gooder, white-girl savior complex grasping for just one small victory to soothe my intense need to be needed: to know that I can save somebody and something.

Jesus faced a similar temptation to seize power to set things straight, once and for all. Before starting his ministry, Jesus went to the wilderness to fast, pray, and discern his course of action (Matt. 4:1–11).[2]

Satan found him there and offered to be his advisor. Imagine, if you will, that Satan offered to serve as the campaign manager to Jesus' Messianic candidacy. A number of leaders claimed to be the savior as the people chafed under Rome. It seems Satan offered to coach Jesus on how to win his contest with Rome.

Satan's first thought was to buy everyone off with material goods (Matt. 4:3). "If you are the Son of God, command these stones to become loaves of bread." Offer the people material comfort and peace will come. Buy them off with strong stock market returns, real estate ventures, military contracts, tax breaks, cheap goods, and credit cards, and all will be well.[3]

Jesus knowingly responded that humanity cannot live by bread alone, but by the word of God (Matt. 4:4). Empires notoriously placate the poor with scraps (bread) and elites with riches. Jesus was after peace of a different nature, origin, and outcome. Material gain works for a quick hit, but never fulfills. Until we learn to love God and others, we will never be at peace.

His first plan rejected, Satan advised Jesus to throw himself off the Temple to show his command of God's angels. Jesus rejected the use of spectacle and ideology to charm the people into submission and confidence (Matt. 4:7). He replied he will not "put God to the test." The people would need to learn to trust God without the advantage of absolute certainty that miracles and pageantry give us. Our desire to turn God into a slot machine—offerings in, spiritual power out—reduces God to an idol to be controlled. Susan Brooks Thistlethwaite observes, "We have to confront the fact that despite being a movement of

God, God does not always show up in the way we might want, exactly when we want. You can die in the wilderness."[4] This is the rejection of God as a god of certainty, who can be told what to do.

Finally Satan goes big. People will never be able to make moral choices that make for peace. In Matthew 4:8, Satan says he will give Jesus "the kingdoms of the world and their splendor," if he worships Satan, the force behind imperial Rome. Instead of *Pax Romana*, we could have *Pax* Jesus. Oust these oppressive Romans by force and put you and your people in power. This was the nationalistic path to power.

Jesus responds, "Worship only God," not Satan, the representative of secular power or the way of the world. Jesus rejects the offer to rule as a king, to be a David or a Solomon.

In many respects, the temptations are a "do over" of the Exodus, Sinai, and Solomonic experience. Jesus is in the wilderness for forty days and the Israelites wandered in the desert for forty years. Jesus does not need the riches of Solomon or bread; he does not rely on the spectacle of the Temple, nor will he opt to be a king, using nationalism and military might to rid people of their fear and insecurity. He will not say the words "I alone can fix it," because he knows that only the people together can fix it. Now it was time to write the law on their hearts—not through miracles or kingships—but by overcoming the desire for control and domination, once and for all. God's liberation ethic would be the only way forward.

This juncture in our nation's history is a chance for a do over. Once we were a land with a great vision—a government for and by the people, driven by an ethic of treating all with human dignity. That vision was derailed from the start by America's original sin of slavery. Movements rose up, and each time they made headway, but never fully prevailed in large part because even those freedom movements denied some their dignity while embracing others. The Civil War ended slavery, but the Compromise of 1877 brought peace without justice by withdrawing federal troops from the South, ending Reconstruction, and putting white supremacy back in office. White suffragists obtained the right to vote by appeasing white Southerners, dismantling Sojourner Truth's dream of a unified bloc of Black and white women voters.

And so here we are again. Can we resist the temptation to grab power, material wealth, the ideological upper hand? Or will we put our faith in kings, in power over others? Will we gain power for some at the expense of others? Will we compromise to keep the peace? And as individuals, can we trust God and step forward in faith to build a new America?

Having seen change happening in Black Lives Matter Plaza, John Lewis's final charge to us was this: "Democracy is not a state. It is an act, and each generation must do its part to help build what we called the Beloved Community, a nation and world society at peace with itself."[5]

God gave us a radical vision that we could create that world—that God, working in us, will lead us to a new earth, where justice rolls down like waters and righteousness like an everlasting stream. But it's not by might as the world gives. And it is not done in certainty, but by having faith in the hope God has given us in Scripture. It's done by all of us, contributing in the ways God has called us to. All of us, doing our work.

Maybe what lies ahead is not the darkness of the tomb, as my friend Valarie Kaur says, maybe this transition is the darkness of the womb. The transition phase of a delivery of a newborn is the toughest phase of all. Transition is when you shut down, lose your mind, give up hope, cry out in despair. But after that, you breathe and push. New life comes out screaming in hope and pain, taking its first breath.

Maybe what we feel now is the spirit of creation, hovering again over darkness of the waters, ready, with us, for a new creation.

Only by seeing who we truly are as a nation can we start afresh. For many of us, our eyes are now open. We see with new clarity what we have to do and where we have to go.

In the time of the prophet Isaiah, the Northern Kingdom had been destroyed and the people of Judea carried off into exile. With no reason in the world to hope, Isaiah heard a new word from God:

> *"Behold, I am doing a new thing; now it springs forth, do you not perceive it? I will make a way in the wilderness and rivers in the desert."* (Isa. 43:19)

Everything had been stripped from Israel. Its Temple, its horses and chariots, its glory—all destroyed. The people's trust in each other stripped away by inequality that stemmed from elite investment in worldly wealth rather than covenant neighborliness. Solomon had even allowed worship of Moloch, who demanded child sacrifice—the sacrifice of children for worldly gain. Into this spiritual void marches the prophet who tells us God will do a new thing.

God is making a way in the wilderness—and it's happening through the cries and footsteps of those calling for a reckoning with democracy.

The question for us is not: Will it happen? The question at hand for us is this: Can we see it? Can we see it in the communion of saints who came before and go after us? Can we catch the current of liberation that runs through this handbook for resisting tyranny we call the Bible? Can we see it in the voices of those crying, calling, and singing out around us?

If so, what a joy it will be for you and all of us to march with God in this radical new charge to humanity. Take heart that a revelation as deep as our brokenness and as high as our potential has drawn back the veil. A new thing can now be done.

RESOURCES

I've explored how Christianity is an antidote to the rise of autocracy as well as how Christianity has been hijacked to serve empire and tyranny. I've introduced concepts that intersect with theology, biblical studies, activism, spirituality, and politics. Below is a list of books in those fields that will help you go deeper and that cover far more than I am able to in this book. Many of these authors have multiple works that would be useful in your journey, although I did not list all of them. These only scratch the surface of what is out there. I hope they get you started. Welcome to the movement. You are not alone!

Liberation Theologies
Gustavo Gutiérrez, *A Theology of Liberation, On Job, God of Life*
Leonardo Boff, *Cry of the Earth, Cry of the Poor*
Jon Sobrino, *Spirituality of Liberation, Christ the Liberator*
Justo Gonzalez, *For the Healing of the Nations* (short and yet extraordinarily profound)
Kelly Brown Douglas, *The Black Christ*
Dr. James Cone, *The Cross and the Lynching Tree*
Howard Thurman, *Jesus for the Disinherited*
Dietrich Bonhœffer, *The Cost of Discipleship*
Delores Williams, *Sisters in the Wilderness: The Challenge of Womanist God Talk*
Katie Cannon, *Katie's Canon: Womanism and the Soul of the Black Community*
Ada Maria Asasi-Diaz, *Mujerista Theology: A Theology for the Twenty-First Century*
Kaetlyn Curtis, *Native: Identity, Belonging, and Discovering God*
Mihee Kim-Kort, *Outside the Lines: How Embracing Queerness Will Transform Your Faith*
Mary Daly, *Beyond God the Father*
Rosemary Radford Reuther, *Sexism and God-Talk: Toward a*

Feminist Theology
The Mission, movie, 1986, Roland Joffé
Romero, movie, 2018, John Duigan
Silence, movie, 2016, Martin Scorcese

Biblical Studies
Rob Bell and Don Golden, *Jesus Wants to Save Christians: Learning to Read a Dangerous Book* see also "Robcast" episodes in 2020
Elsa Tamez, *Bible of the Oppressed*
Rachel Held Evans, *Inspired: Slaying Giants, Walking on Water,* and *Loving the Bible Again*
Phillis Trible, *Texts of Terror: Literary-Feminist Readings of Biblical Narratives*
Jeremiah Unterman, *Justice for All: How the Jewish Bible Revolutionized Ethics*
Liz Theoharis, *Always with Us?: What Jesus Really Said about the Poor*
Lisa Sharon Harper, *The Very Good Gospel: How Everything Wrong Can Be Made Right*
Matthew Vines, *God and the Gay Christian: The Biblical Case in Support of Same Sex Relationships*

Faith and Activism
Guthrie Grave Fitzsimmons, *Just Faith: Reclaiming Progressive Christianity*
Rev. William Barber, *We Are Called to Be a Movement*
Jack Jenkins, *American Prophets: The Religious Roots of Progressive Politics and the Ongoing Fight for the Soul of the Country*

Progressive Activism and Spirituality
Brian McLaren, *The Great Spiritual Migration: How the World's Largest Religion Is Seeking a Better Way to Be Christian*
Richard Rohr, *The Universal Christ: How a Forgotten Reality Can*

Change Everything We See, Hope for, and Believe
Simone Campbell, *Hunger for Hope: Prophetic Communities, Contemplation, and the Common Good*
Ruth King, *Mindful of Race: Transforming Racism from the Inside Out*

Understanding Authoritarianism, Democracy, Fascism, White Supremacy, Christian Right/Nationalism
Christian Liberation v. Christian Authoritarianism
Rita Brock, *Saving Paradise: How Christianity Traded Love of this World for Crucifixion and Empire*
Diana Butler Bass, *A People's History of Christianity: The Other Side of History*
Julie Engersoll, *Building God's Kingdom* (traces roots of authoritarianism in Christian Right movements)
Jonathan Wilson Hargrove, *Revolution of Values: Reclaiming Faith for the Common Good*
Elizabeth Phillips, *Political Theology for the Perplexed*

Christian Nationalism
Andrew Whitehead and Samuel Perry, *Taking America Back for God: Christian Nationalism in the United States*
Christians Against Christian Nationalism campaign, https://bjconline.org/christiannationalism/

Autocracy/Fascism
Steven Levitsky and Daniel Ziblatt, *How Democracies Die*
Timothy Snyder, *On Tyranny: Lessons from the Twentieth Century*
Charles Marsh, *Strange Glory: A Life of Dietrich Bonhœffer*

Books that tackle idolatries we've been taught
Rob Bell, *Love Wins* (a book for anyone who grew up in a HellFire Damnation type theology)
Rafael Warnock, *The Divided Mind of the Black Church:*

Theology, Piety, and Public Witness (Religion, Race, and Ethnicity)

Susan Thistletwhaite, *Occupy the Bible: What Jesus Really Said (and Did) about Money and Power*

Kathy Khang, *Raise Your Voice: Why We Stay Silent and How to Speak Up*

Notes to the Introduction

1. For an excellent review of these rollbacks, read Carol Anderson, *White Rage: The Unspoken Truth of Our Racial Divide*. New York: Bloomsbury USA; (May 31, 2016)

2. https://www.cbpp.org/research/poverty-and-inequality/a-guide-to-statistics-on-historical-trends-in-income-inequality

3. FAIR is a nonprofit organization that tracks media bias on the left and the right. For more information, see: https://fair.org/about-fair/whats-wrong-with-the-news/

4. Jane Mayer, *Dark Money: The Hidden History of the Billionaires Behind the Rise of the Radical Right*. New York: Anchor; (January 24, 2017)

5. I use uppercase "Black" to describe people and cultures of African origin, both in the United States and elsewhere. This style best conveys elements of shared history and identity.

6. A group of South Carolinians advocating secession explained in 1861, "We detest Abolitionism because it trespasses upon our rights of conscience. It does not allow us to judge for ourselves the morality of slaveholding." https://reflections.yale.edu/article/future-race/american-religious-freedom-pride-and-prejudice

7. https://www.epi.org/blog/who-are-essential-workers-a-comprehensive-look-at-their-wages-demographics-and-unionization-rates/

8. https://www.vox.com/2018/11/5/18059454/trump-white-evangelicals-christian-nationalism-john-fea

9. Charles Marsh, *Strange Glory: A Life of Dietrich Bonhœffer*. New York: First Vintage Books, 2015

10. https://religionnews.com/2018/11/27/museum-highlights-slave-bible-that-focuses-on-servitude-leaves-out-freedom/

11. *The Narrative of Sojourner Truth*. Introduction and Notes by Imani Perry. New York: Barnes and Noble, 2005. p. xvii

12. *Letter from a Birmingham Jail, Martin Luther King*. Author: King, Martin Luther, Jr. (Southern Christian Leadership Conference) Date: April 16, 1963 Location: Birmingham, Ala. okra.stanford.edu/transcription/document_images/undecided/630416-019.pdf

Notes to Chapter 1

1. Kevin Kruse, *White Flight: Atlanta and the Making of Modern Conservatism*. Princeton, NJ: Princeton University Press, 2005. pp. 161–191
2. http://www.usaschoolinfo.com/school/lovett-school-atlanta-georgia.113754/enrollment#:~:text=The%20student%20body%20of%20Lovett%20School%20in%20Atlanta%2C%20Fulton%20County,-made%20up%20of%207%20ethnicities.&text=This%20is%20followed%20by%20Black,and%20Pacific%20Islander%20(0.1%20%25).
3. https://www.anglicancommunion.org/media/253799/1-What-is-Lectio-Divina.pdf

Notes to Chapter 2

1. https://www.nytimes.com/2007/05/24/arts/24crea.html
2. https://news.gallup.com/poll/261680/americans-believe-creationism.aspx
3. Marduk was the patron god of Babylon. Read more about his mythology here: https://www.ancient.eu/Marduk/
4. Jeremiah Unterman, *Justice for All: How the Jewish Bible Revolutionized Ethics*. Philadelphia: The Jewish Publication Society, 2017. p. 2.
5. Ibid. pp. 2-3
6. Ibid. pp. 3-4
7. Ibid. pp. 4-6
8. Ibid. p. 5
9. Ibid. p. 6
10. https://www.washingtonpost.com/archive/opinions/1989/03/26/genesis-from-eves-point-of-view/dc371184-1f4c-4142-ac2d-d5efee-72a0da/
11. Ibid. (Jeremiah Unterman, *Justice for All*). p. 7
12. Ibid. (Jeremiah Unterman, *Justice for All*). p. 29
13. https://www.washingtonpost.com/opinions/sister-norma-wanted-to-show-trump-what-it-is-like-on-the-border-he-didnt-care-to-listen/2019/01/11/99fa6da8-15e1-11e9-803c-4ef28312c8b9_story.html
14. https://www.washingtonpost.com/opinions/2019/01/10/welcome-border-mr-president/

15. https://news.wttw.com/2018/12/26/new-book-explores-jewish-roots-progressive-views

16. https://www.counter-currents.com/2013/07/why-christiani-ty-cant-save-us/

17. Andrew L. Whitehead and Samuel L. Perry, *Taking America Back for God: Christian Nationalism in the United States.* New York: Oxford University Press, 2020. p. 10.

Notes to Chapter 3

1. Rob Bell and Don Golden, *Jesus Wants to Save Christians: Learning to Read a Dangerous Book.* New York: Harper One, 2012. p. 186

2. Ibid.

3. Rosemary Radford Ruether, *Sexism and God-Talk: Toward a Feminist Theology.* Boston: Beacon Press, 1983. p. 66

4. Paulo Freire in *Pedagogy of the Oppressed.* New York: Continuum, 2003. pp. 57–58.

5. Martin Buber, quoted in Nahum Ward-Lev, *The Liberating Path of the Hebrew Prophets: Then and Now.* New York: Orbis, 2019. pp. 123–125.

6. Ibid. p. 128

7. Ibid. Chapter 3

8. https://www.au.org/church-state/march-2019-church-state-maga-zine/people-events/god-wanted-trump-to-be-president-press

9. Mark Galli. "Trump Should be Removed from Office," *Christianity Today.* December 19, 2019 https://www.christianitytoday.com/ct/2019/december-web-only/trump-should-be-removed-from-office.html

Notes to Chapter 4

1. Ibid. (Nahum Ward-Lev, *The Liberating Path of the Hebrew Prophets*)

2. Steven Levitsky and Daniel Ziblatt, *How Democracies Die.* New York: Broadway Books, 2018

3. Ibid. p. 5

4. Ibid. pp. 61–71

5. https://www.nytimes.com/1979/03/27/archives/censorship-of-text-books-is-found-on-rise-in-schools-around-nation.html

6. Timothy Snyder, *The Road to Unfreedom: Russia, Europe, America*. New York: Tim Duggan Books, 2018. pp. 7–8

7. Jack Jenkins, *American Prophets: The Religious Roots of Progressive Politics and the Ongoing Fight for the Soul of the Country*. New York: HarperOne, 2020. p. 88

8. Ibid.

9. https://www.npr.org/sections/thetwo-way/2017/05/15/528457693/supreme-court-declines-republican-bid-to-revive-north-carolina-voter-id-law

10. https://www.politico.com/story/2013/05/koch-brothers-republicans-north-carolina-091200

11. Ibid. (Jack Jenkins, *American Prophets*). p. 77

12. Ibid. (Jack Jenkins, *American Prophets*). p. 82

13. https://www.aclu.org/news/civil-liberties/block-the-vote-voter-suppression-in-2020/

14. https://www.prwatch.org/news/2011/11/11117/koch-funded-alec-agenda-works-deny-voting-rights-brave-new-film-highlights-voter-

15. Rev. Dr. William J. Barber II and Jonathan Wilson-Hartgrove, *The Third Reconstruction: How a Moral Movement Is Overcoming the Politics of Division and Fear*. Boston: Beacon Press, 2016

Notes to Chapter 5

1. Ibid. (Rob Bell and Don Golden, Jesus Wants to Save Christians). Pp 29-30.

2. Great summary of all the related verses here as well: https://bibleproject.com/blog/solomon-love-hate/

3. Ibid. Rob Bell and Don Golden, p. 31-37

4. Walter Brueggemann, *The Prophetic Imagination*, Second Edition. Minneapolis: Augsburg Fortress, 2001. Chapter 2

5. Ibid. (Timothy Snyder, *The Road to Unfreedom*). p. 7

6. Ibid. (Timothy Snyder, *The Road to Unfreedom*). p. 35

7. Ibid. (Carol Anderson, *White Rage*). p. 5

8. For details on Robert Jeffress' sermons and how they relate to

Christian nationalism see Andrew L. Whitehead and Samuel L. Perry, *Taking America Back for God: Christian Nationalism in the United States*. New York: Oxford University Press, 2020.

9. Ibid. (Walter Brueggemann, *The Prophetic Imagination*, Second Edition). p. 45

10. Ibid. (Walter Brueggemann, *The Prophetic Imagination*, Second Edition). pp. 45–46.

11. *Washington Post* (video) in 'This can't be happening': An oral history of 48 surreal, violent, biblical minutes in Washington, Video: Washington <iframe width='480' height='290' scrolling='no' src='https://www.washingtonpost.com/video/c/embed/7d-7f505b-7079-4a86-beab-4c08692a5fe7' frameborder='0' webkitallowfullscreen mozallowfullscreen allowfullscreen></iframe>n Post

12. https://www.washingtonpost.com/local/episcopal-priest-describes-being-gassed-and-overrun-by-police-at-lafayette-square-church/2020/06/02/c5dbb282-a4ed-11ea-bb20-ebf0921f3bbd_story.html

13. https://www.washingtonpost.com/lifestyle/style/this-cant-be-happening-an-oral-history-of-48-surreal-violent-biblical-minutes-in-washington/2020/06/02/6683d36e-a4e3-11ea-b619-3f9133bbb482_story.html

14. MSNBC, Sunday May 31, 8:17 PM

Notes to Chapter 6

1. Ibid. (Rosemary Radford Reuther, *Sexism and God-Talk*). pp. 153–156.

2. Soraya Chemaly, *Rage Becomes Her: The Power of Women's Anger*. New York: Atria, 2018. p. 103

3. https://action.groundswell-mvmt.org/petitions/pro-life-evangelicals-call-for-a-pause-in-culture-war

4. Jerry Falwell and Oral Roberts were running private Christian academies that denied entry to Black students. The U.S. Supreme Court ruled that they would lose their tax-free status if they discriminated. Under the guise of "religious freedom," Jerry Falwell, and now his son, Jerry Falwell Jr., claimed they had a religious right to

discriminate. In a sermon called "Segregation or Integration: Which?" Falwell preached: "If Chief Justice Warren and his associates had known God's word and had desired to do the Lord's will, I am quite confident that the 1954 decision would never have been made. The facilities should be separate. When God has drawn a line of distinction, we should not attempt to cross that line...."

5. https://www.usatoday.com/story/opinion/voices/2019/05/15/alabama-ohio-abortion-heartbeat-restrictions-choice-column/3679623002/

6. https://www.washingtonpost.com/news/retropolis/wp/2017/11/08/transgender-people-have-been-elected-before-but-they-can-finally-let-the-voters-know/

Notes to Chapter 7

1. Special Counsel Robert S. Mueller III, Report on the Investigation into Russian Interference in the 2016 Election, Volume I or II. Submitted Pursuant to 28 C.F.R 600.8 c, Washington, DC, March 2019. pp. 14–15; pp. 24–25

2. https://www.nytimes.com/2018/03/10/opinion/sunday/youtube-politics-radical.html

3. https://www.nytimes.com/2018/09/07/world/europe/youtube-far-right-extremism.html

4. John Dominic Crossan, Who Killed Jesus?: Exposing the Roots of Anti-Semitism in the Gospel Story of the Death of Jesus. San Francisco: HarperOne, 1st Edition; (February 2, 1996). p. 149

5. Warren Carter, "Matthew Negotiates the Roman Empire," in Richard A. Horsley, In the Shadow of Empire: Reclaiming the Bible as a History of Faithful Resistance. Louisville, KY: Westminster John Knox Press, 2008. pp.124–127

6. https://www.washingtonpost.com/politics/2019/12/16/president-trump-has-made-false-or-misleading-claims-over-days/

7. Ibid. (Timothy Snyder, The Road to Unfreedom). p. 67

8. Ibid. (Steven Levitsky and Daniel Ziblatt, How Democracies Die). pp. 146–149

9. https://www.washingtonpost.com/politics/2019/04/25/

meet-trump-charlottesville-truthers/

10. https://www.washingtonpost.com/news/book-party/ wp/2015/06/17/how-donald-trump-plays-the-press-in-his-own-words/

11. Ibid. (Charles Marsh, Strange Glory). p. 160

12. Ibid. (Charles Marsh, Strange Glory). p. 269

Notes to Chapter 8

1. William Still's book *The Underground Railroad* (1872) is one of the most important historical records we have of escaped slaves. Although Still recognized the many contributions of white abolitionists, he portrayed the fugitives as courageous individuals who struggled for their own freedom.

2. Cherice Bock, "Romans 12:17–13:10 & Quakers' Relation to the State," *Quaker Religious Thought: Vol. 116, Article 2*, 2011. Available at: https://digitalcommons.georgefox.edu/qrt/vol116/iss1/2

3. Ibid. (Cherice Bock, "Quakers' Relation to the State"). p. 8

4. Ibid. (Cherice Bock, "Quakers' Relation to the State"). p. 15

5. J.H. Yoder, *The Politics of Jesus*. Grand Rapids, MI: Eerdmans Publishing Co., 1972. pp. 207–208, p. 211

6. Ibid. (Jack Jenkins, *American Prophets*). pp. 138–139

Notes to Chapter 9

1. https://reflections.yale.edu/article/end-times-and-end-gamesis-scripture-being-left-behind/give-me-end-time-religion

2. https://www.neh.gov/humanities/2017/winter/feature/the-late-great-planet-earth-made-the-apocalypse-popular-concern

3. Jennifer Butler, *Born Again: The Christian Right Globalized*. Ann Arbor, MI: University of Michigan Press, 2006

4. https://www.washingtonpost.com/religion/2020/03/17/not-end-of-the-world-coronavirus-bible-prophecy/

5. Ibid. (Greg Carey, "The Book of Revelation as CounterImperial Script," in Richard A. Horsley, *In the Shadow of Empire*). p.163

6. Liz Theoharis, *Always with Us? What Jesus Really Said about the Poor*. Grand Rapids, MI: Eerdmans Publishing Co., 2017. p. 91

7. Brian K. Blount, *Can I Get a Witness?: Reading Revelation through*

African American Culture. Louisville, KY: Westminster John Knox Press, 2005. p. 46; Ibid. (Greg Carey, "The Book of Revelation as CounterImperial Script," in Richard A Horsley, *In the Shadow of Empire*). p.173

8. Ibid. (Delores Williams quoted in Brian K. Blount, *Can I Get a Witness?*). p. 77

9. Ibid. (Brian K. Blount, *Can I Get a Witness?*). p. 87

10. Austin Channing Brown, *I'm Still Here: Black Dignity in a World Made for Whiteness.* New York: Convergent, 2018. pp. 178–180

11. Ibid.

12. Rebecca Solnit, *Hope in the Dark: Untold Histories, Wild Possibilities.* Chicago: Haymarket Books, 2016. pp 27–28

Notes to the Conclusion

1. https://www.nytimes.com/2020/07/30/opinion/john-lewis-civil-rights-america.html

2. Ibid. (J.H. Yoder, *The Politics of Jesus*). p. 24

3. "Satan's Temptations in Dostœvsky and Tolstoy" by Caleb Upton (Political Theology https://politicaltheology.com/satans-temptations-in-dostœvsky-and-tolstoy-caleb-upton/)

4. Susan Brooks Thistlethwaite, *#Occupy the Bible: What Jesus Really Said (and Did) About Money and Power.* Eugene, OR: Wipf and Stock Publishers, 2012. p. 24

5. https://www.nytimes.com/2020/07/30/opinion/john-lewis-civil-rights-america.html

ACKNOWLEDGMENTS

Many have compared a book to birthing a baby and I would say that is a pretty good analogy. It certainly takes a village. This book took nine months and was written in another year of tumult—a pandemic, a racial justice uprising, a failing democracy.

First, I have to thank Dr. Timothy Snyder whose book *On Tyranny: Twenty Lessons from the Twentieth Century* inspired my thinking about how to apply those lessons to faith activism. It was an honor to do a Facebook live with him to explore some of these themes. Bill Gœttler, dean for Ministerial and Professional Leadership at Yale Divinity School, invited me to teach a seminar in the Fall of 2019 and asked on our way to the airport: "Hey, are you going to turn this into a book?" I had thought, but not dared spoken, of such a dream.

The team at Faith in Public Life could have responded, "Are you kidding me? We have our hands full with this president!" But our all-female leadership team found a way to help me carve out some time. I am particularly grateful for Anna Ibrahim, our fearless Chief of Staff and Chief Organizing Officer, who marched into my office with a plan to free me from the daily onslaught of advocacy campaigns and fundraising to support the work. I am also grateful to Michelle Nealy, Greg Williams, and Dan Nejfelt for their edits and to the whole staff for their work that inspired the lessons within.

Just as the book of Exodus begins with three sets of women organizing against Pharaoh, it was a group of women who kept me going at multiple turning points when I nearly gave up. Susan Barnett of the Auburn Senior Fellows program pushed me on the structure and title, encouraging me to let my voice shine through my writing style. Still working that out, but thanks to her, getting closer. Juliet Vedral helped research and improve early drafts. She helped me see the power of storytelling as one of my strengths. Dr. Susan Thistlethwaite also rescued me from the depths of writing despair telling me I was onto something, sending me outlines, pointers, edits, and critical exegetical material to speed the process. Without the encouragement from these three women I never would have made the deadline, much less published the book.

Then came Cara Highsmith through my friend Brian McLaren. She was an absolute Godsend. Cara brought her long experience with book editing and publishing, helping me bring more uniformity and clarity to the ideas.

I can't thank these folks enough. My life has been a journey to have faith in my own voice and the new thing God is doing in and through me. It has always been communities of women who have led me out of the wilderness of doubt, despair, confusion.

Acknowledgements are about giving thanks, but they also highlight how we are connected to one another. As I say in the book, we walk in the footsteps of the ancestors who got us here and those who will come after us. They may see the promised land even if we don't. I am indebted to these people and more who came ahead of me and whose writings and witness showed me the way. And I am indebted to those of you who find the God of Liberation these pages. May you go forth with the community of saints before and behind you, may you find joy and peace, despite grief, in the work of liberating humanity.

ABOUT THE AUTHOR

Jennifer Butler is the founding executive director of Faith in Public Life (FPL) and the former chair of the White House Council on Faith-based and Neighborhood Partnerships. Before leading FPL, Jennifer spent ten years working in the field of international human rights representing the Presbyterian Church (USA) at the United Nations and is an ordained minister. While mobilizing religious communities to address the AIDS pandemic and advocating for women's rights, she grew passionate about the need to counter religious extremism with a strong religious argument for human rights. Out of that experience, she wrote *Born Again: The Christian Right Globalized*, which was published by University of Michigan Press. That book calls for a progressive religious response to Religious Right efforts to take the culture wars global.

Jennifer served in the Peace Corps from 1989 to 1991 in a Mayan village in Belize, Central America, where she discovered she was a community organizer at heart. A graduate of Princeton Theological Seminary, she also studied public policy and community organizing and graduated with an MSW from Rutgers University. She's a graduate of the College of William & Mary.

Jennifer loves hiking and biking with her family and friends.

For more information visit RevJenButler.com or @RevJenButler on Twitter or @RevJenniferButler on Facebook.

www.faithinpubliclife.org
@FaithPublicLife

Faith in Public Life is a national movement of clergy and faith leaders united in the prophetic pursuit of justice, equality and the common good.

Together, we are leading the fight to advance just policies at the local, state, and federal levels. Our network of 50,000 leaders engage in bold moral action that affirms our values and the human dignity of all. We are committed to racial equity and are on an intentional, transformational, accountable journey toward internally and externally living out these values and deconstructing white supremacy. We envision a world where prophetic faith voices triumph so that justice and democracy prevail and all people live in peace, dignity, community, and abundance.

Please visit **FaithinPublicLife.org** to sign up for information on current activities and join in our work together. Visit us also on Twitter: **@FaithPublicLife**

Printed in the USA
CPSIA information can be obtained
at www.ICGtesting.com
LVHW102025210823
755862LV00011B/255